THANK YOU GOD!

Handwriting Practice Letter Tracing Workbook

THANK YOU GOD! Handwriting Practice Letter Tracing Workbook Copyright
© 2021 by Dr. Diana Carle
Nature's Living Classroom Publishing
For Information Contact:
Dr. Diana Carle at www.DoctorDianaCarle.com
Written and illustrated by Dr. Diana Carle

This Book Belongs to:

_____

The letter A

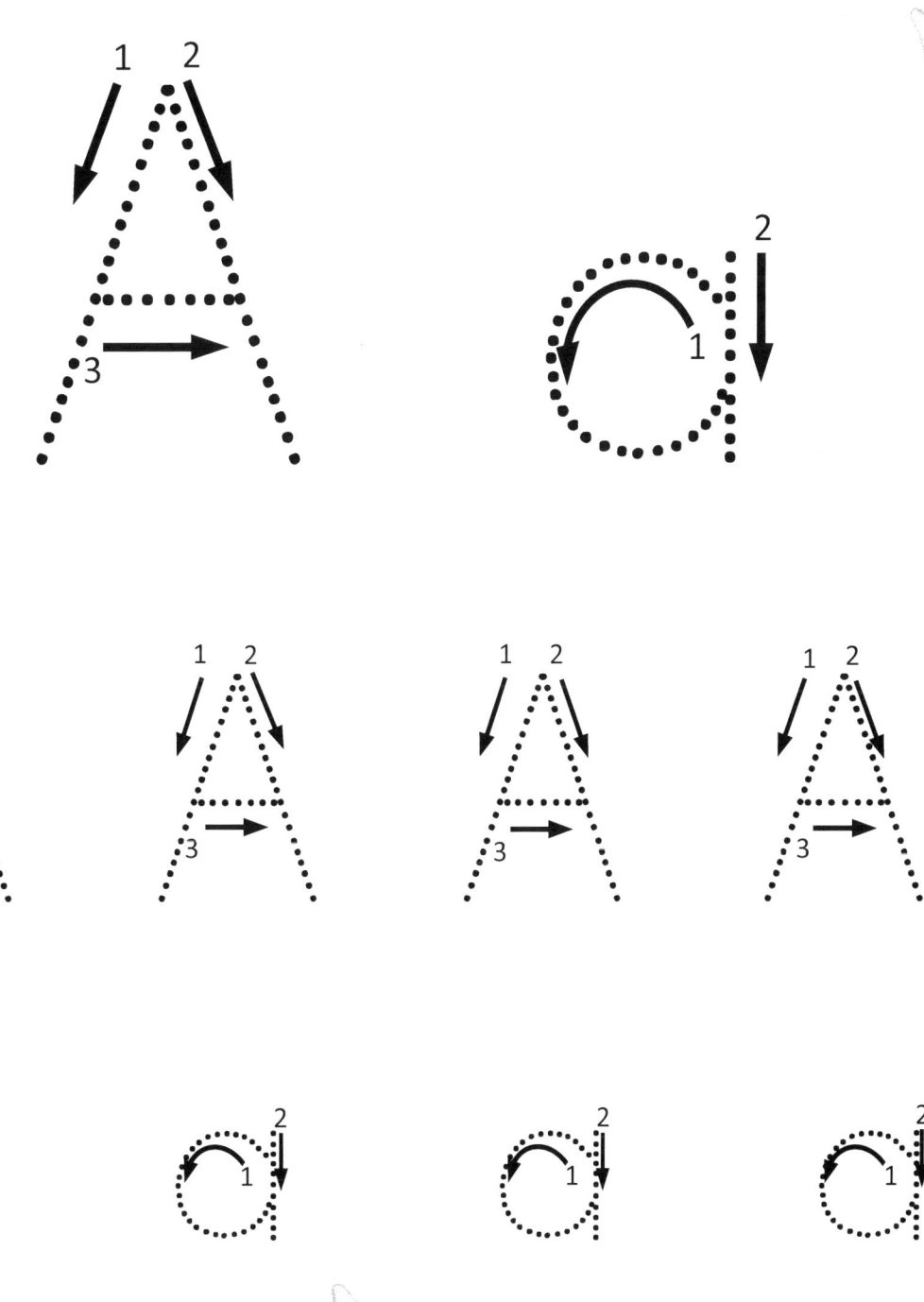

A is for Apple!

Thank You God for Apples!

Apple

The letter B

B is for Bee!

Thank You God for Bees!

Bee

The letter C

C is for Carrot!
Thank You God for Carrots!

Carrot

The letter D

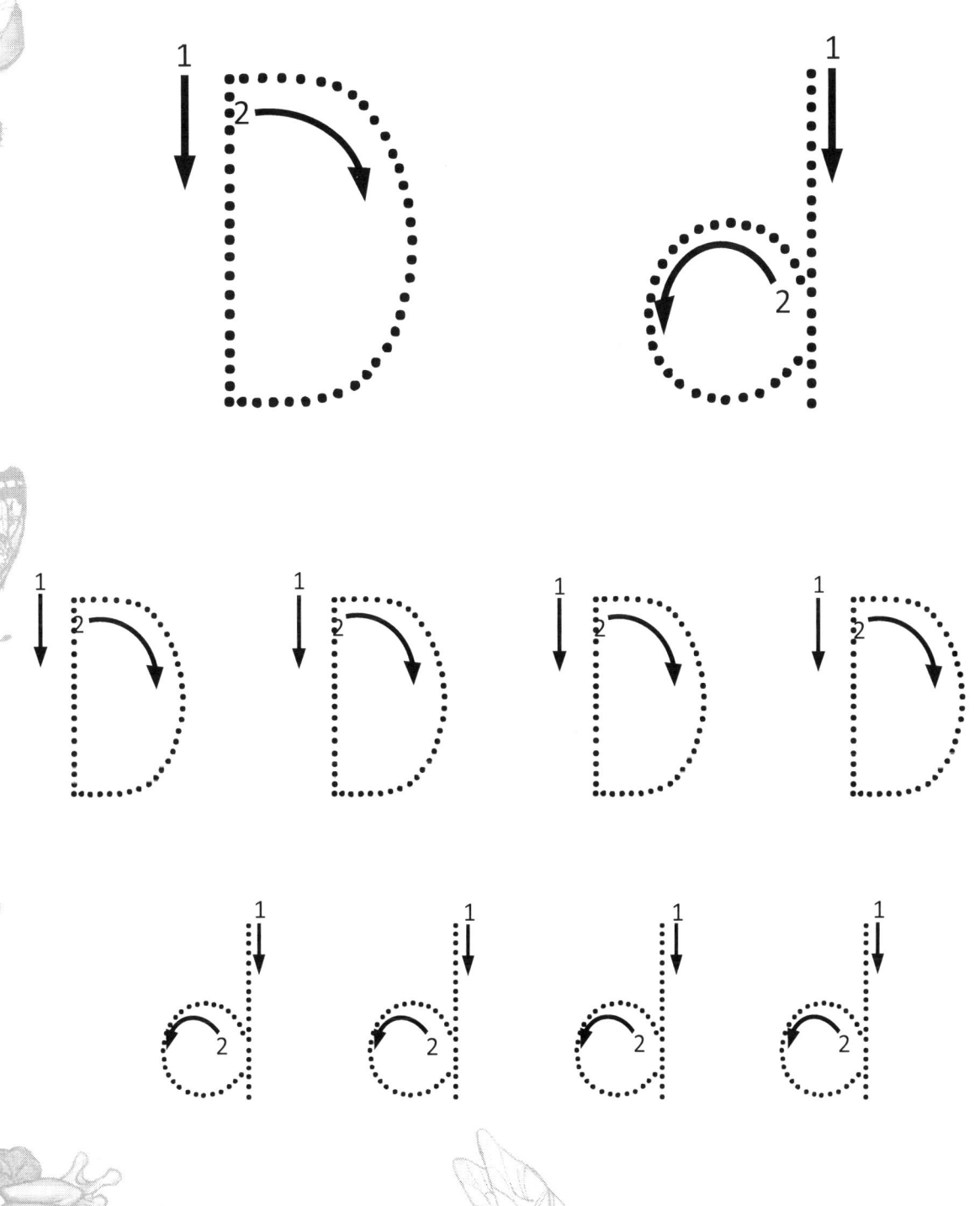

D is for Deer!

Thank You God for Deer!

Deer

The letter E

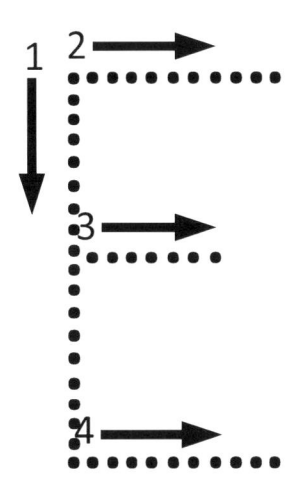 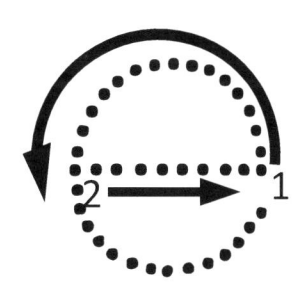

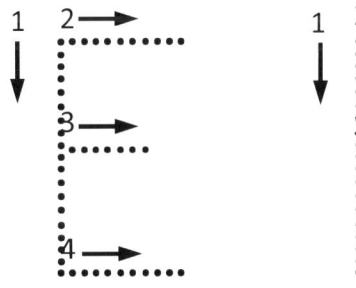 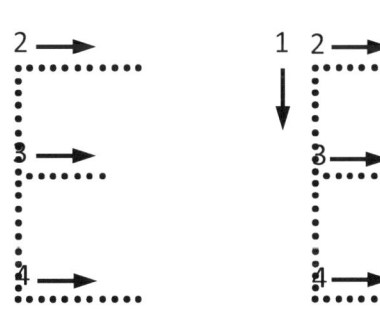 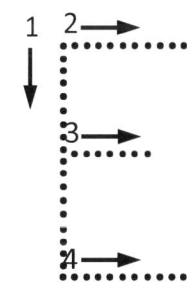

E is for Egg!

Thank You God for Eggs!

Egg

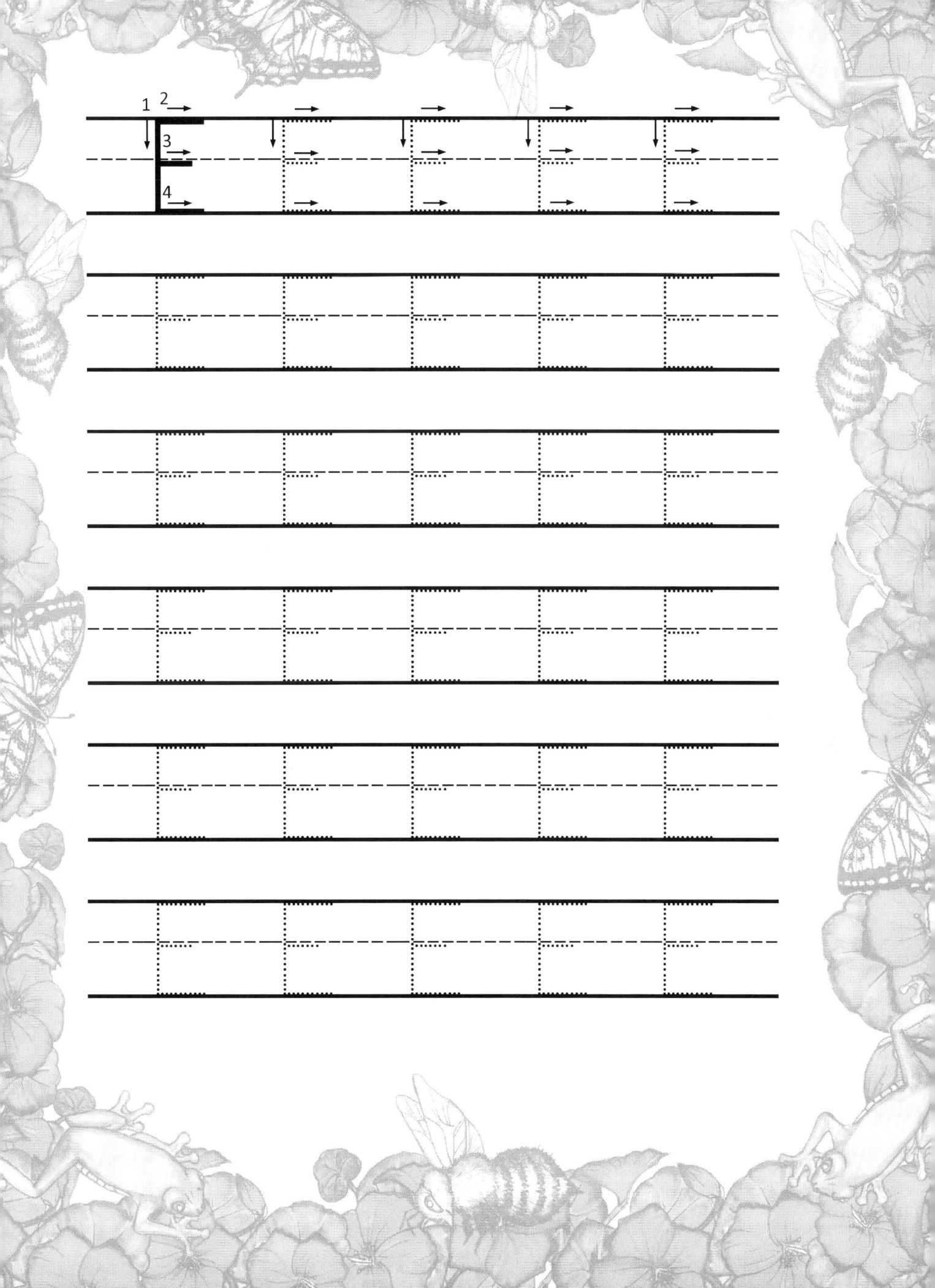

The letter F

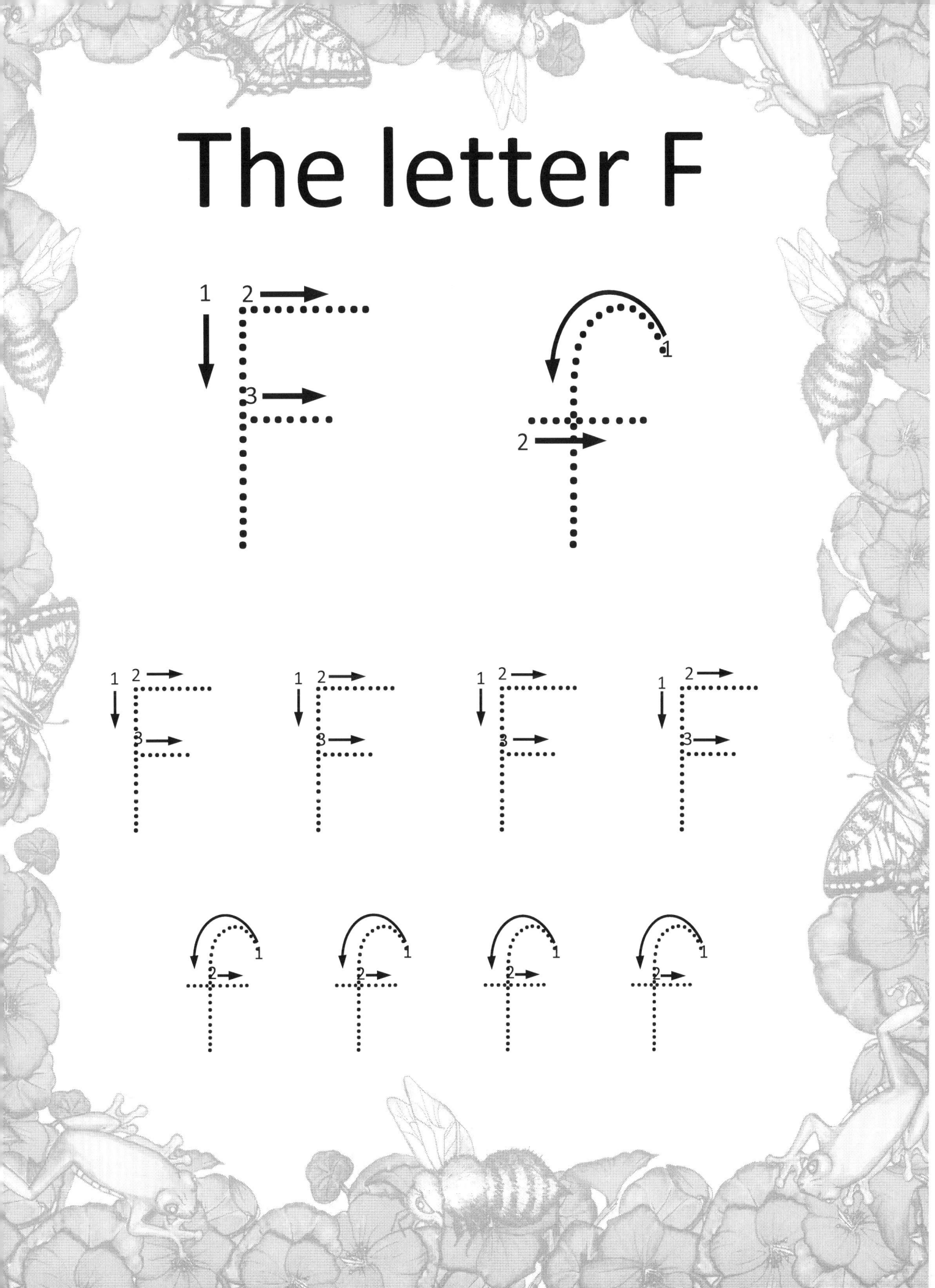

F is for Frog!

Thank You God for Frogs!

Frog

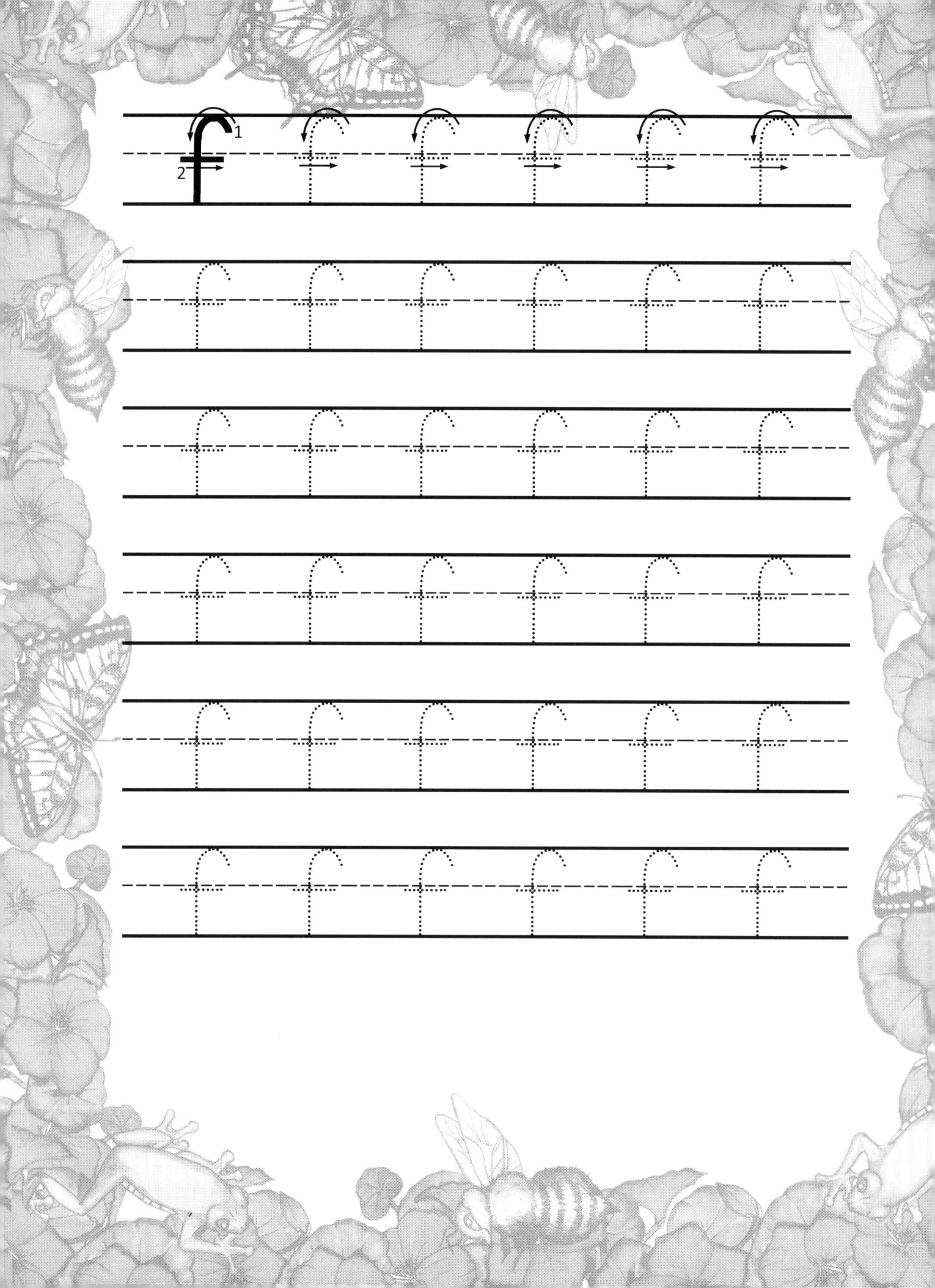

The letter G

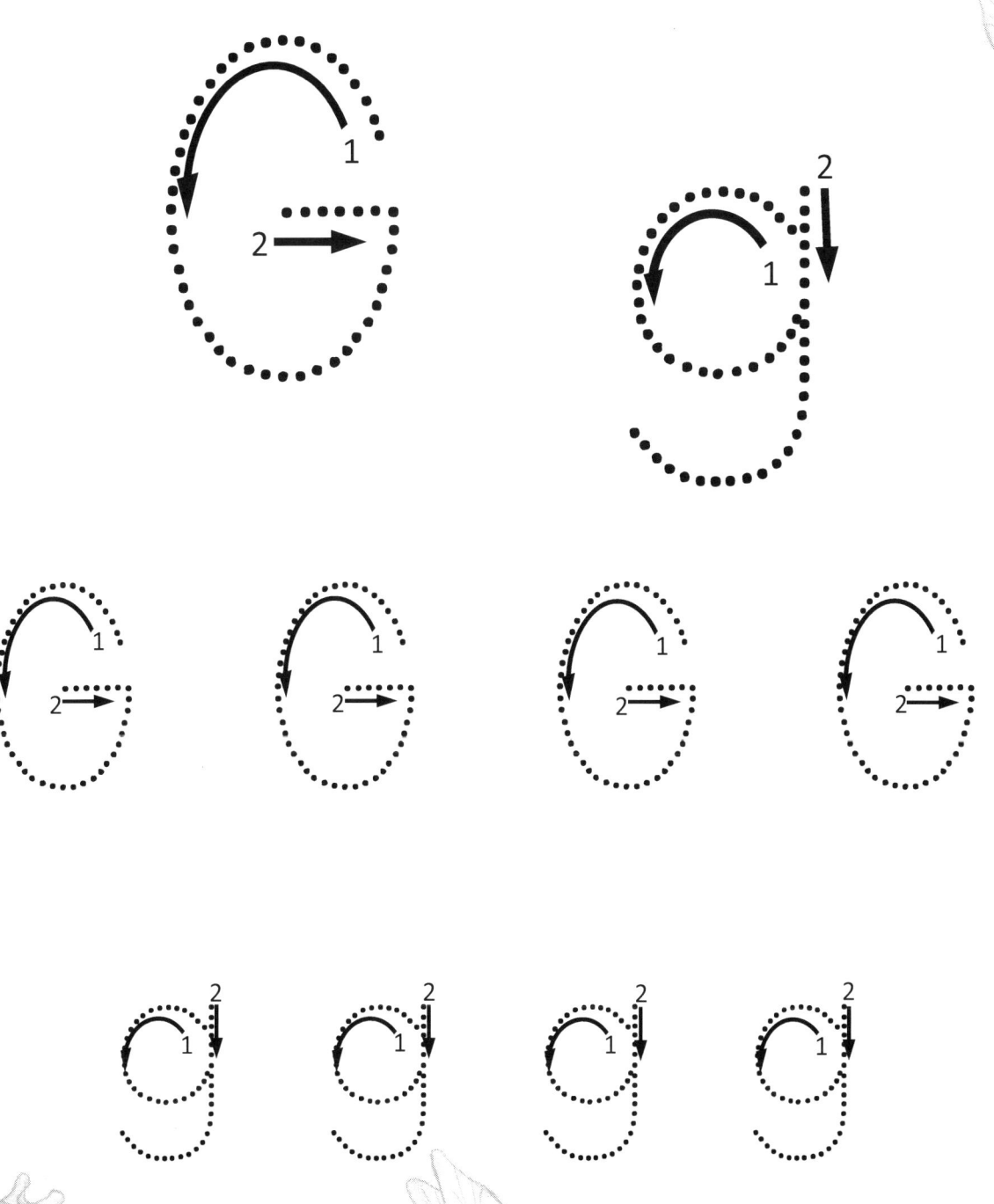

G is for Garden!

Thank You God for Gardens!

Garden

The letter H

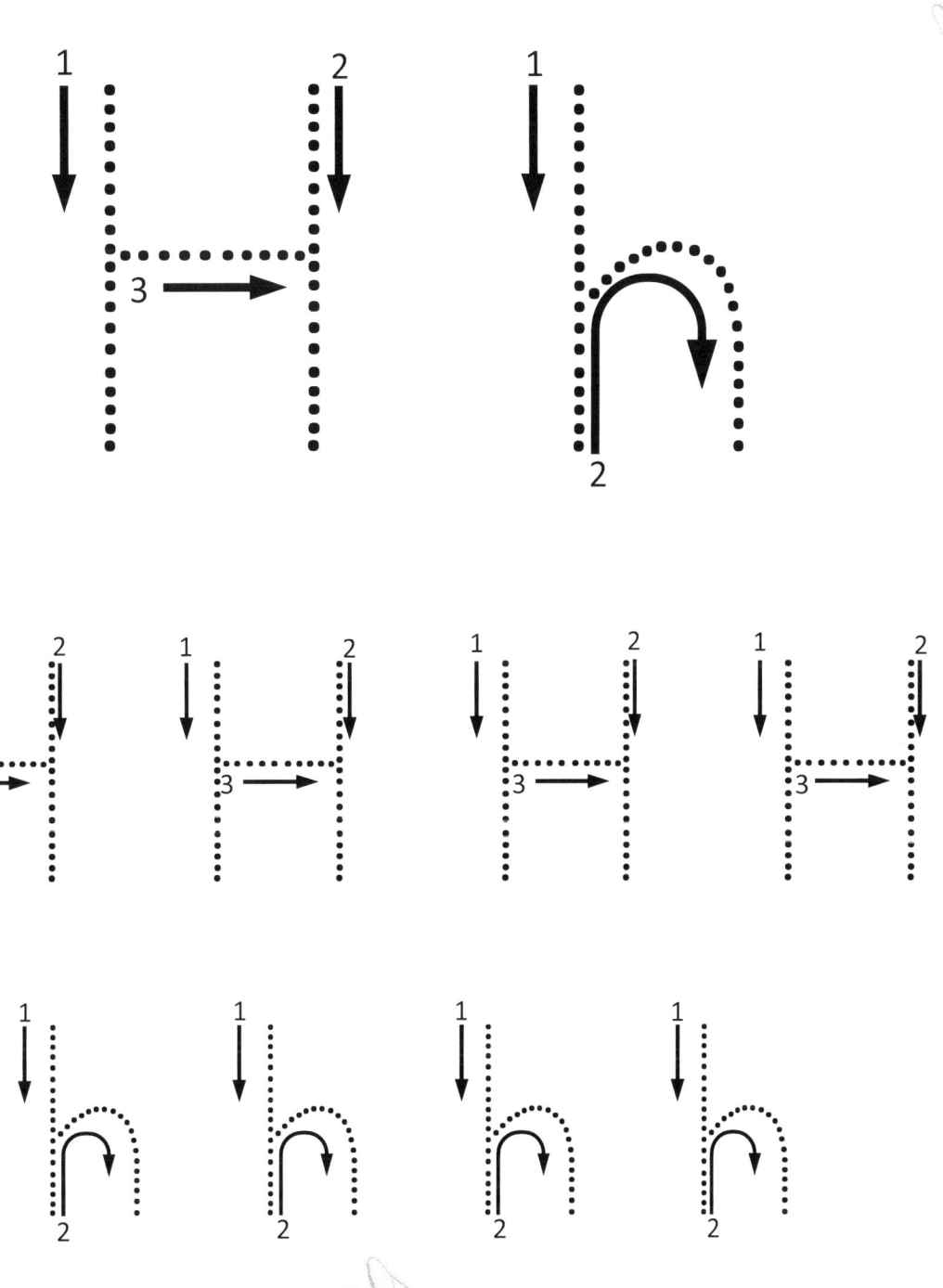

H is for Heart!

Thank You God for Hearts!

Heart

The letter I

I is for Insect!

Thank You God for Insects!

Insect

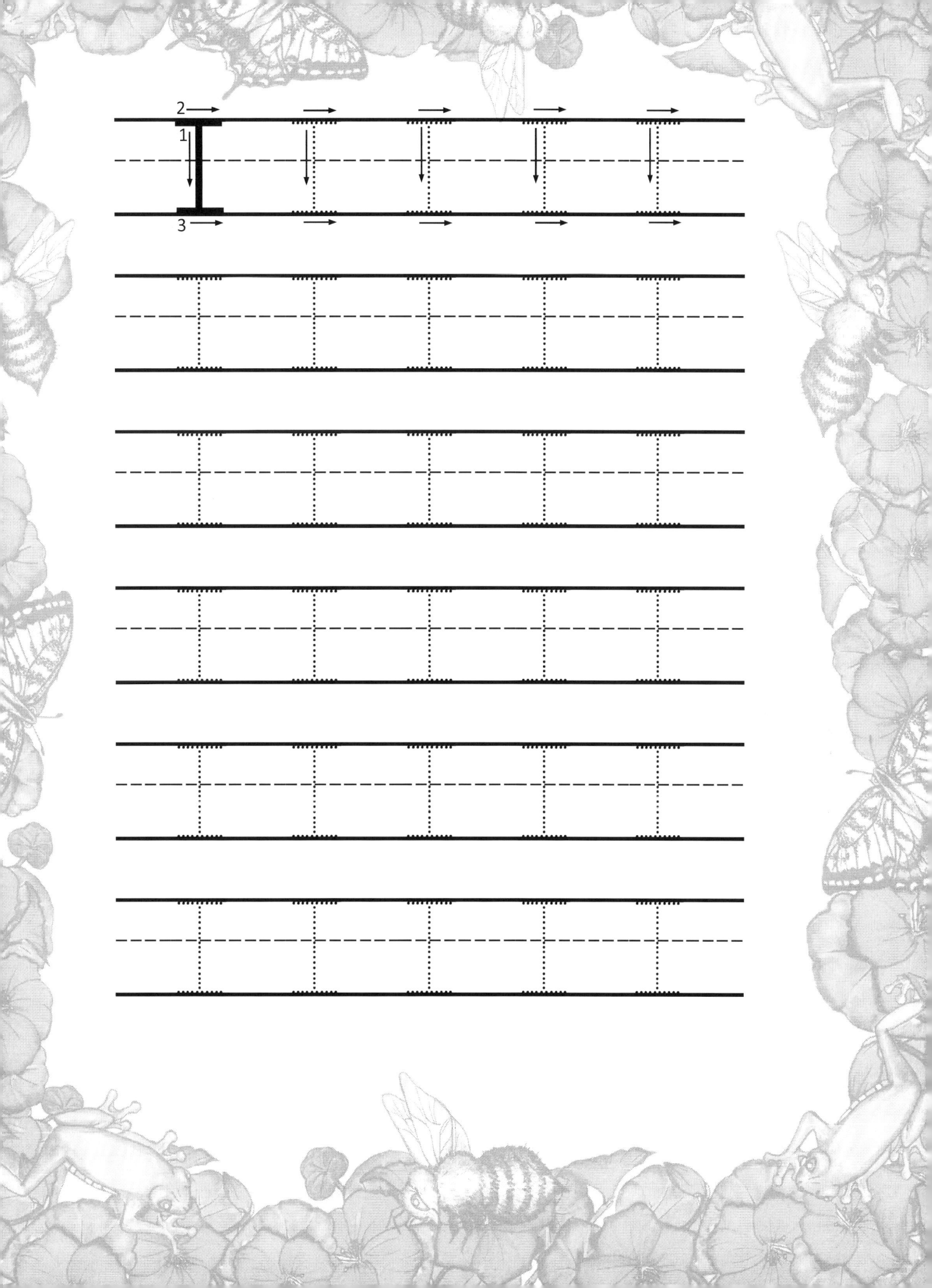

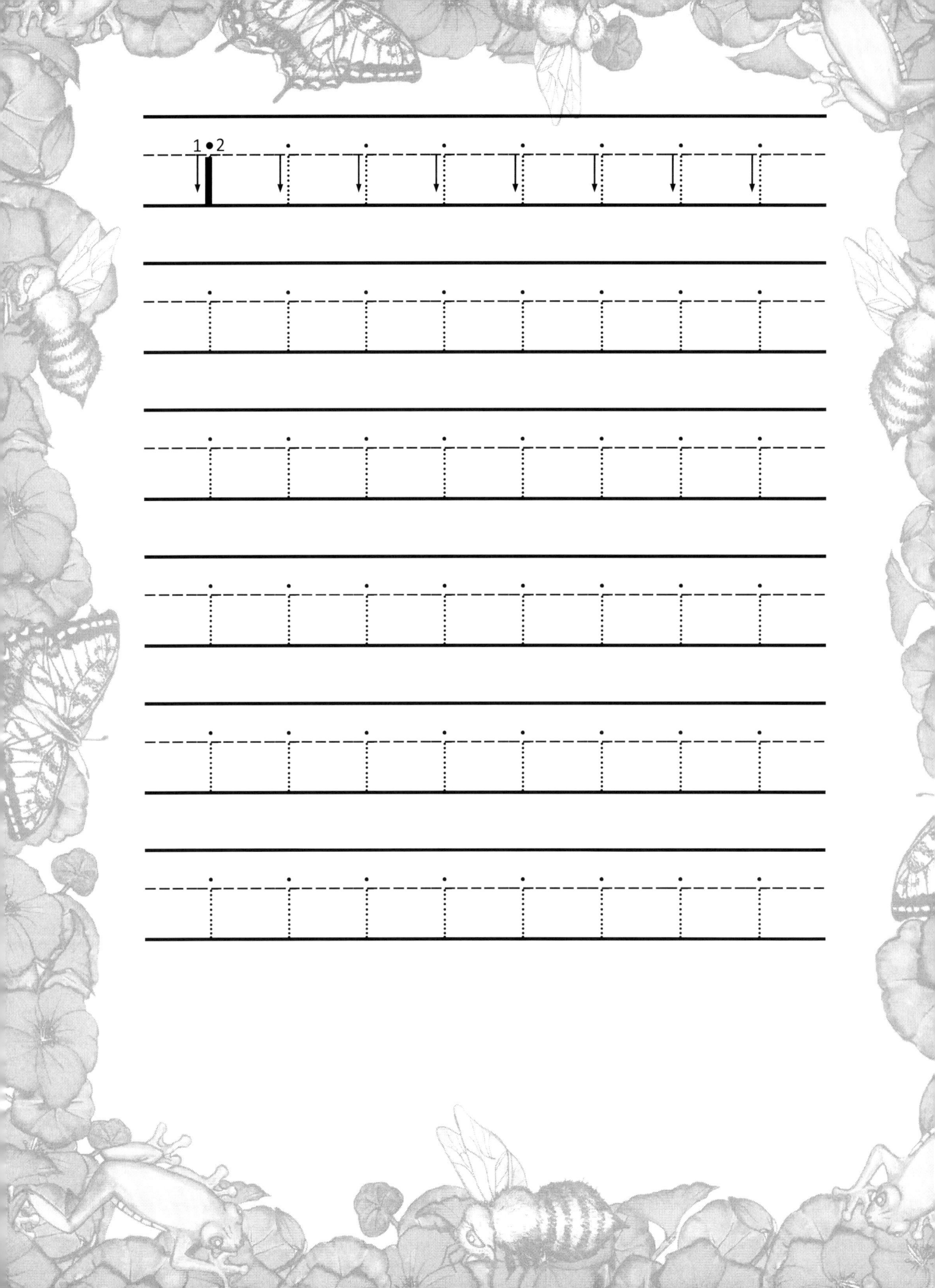

The letter J

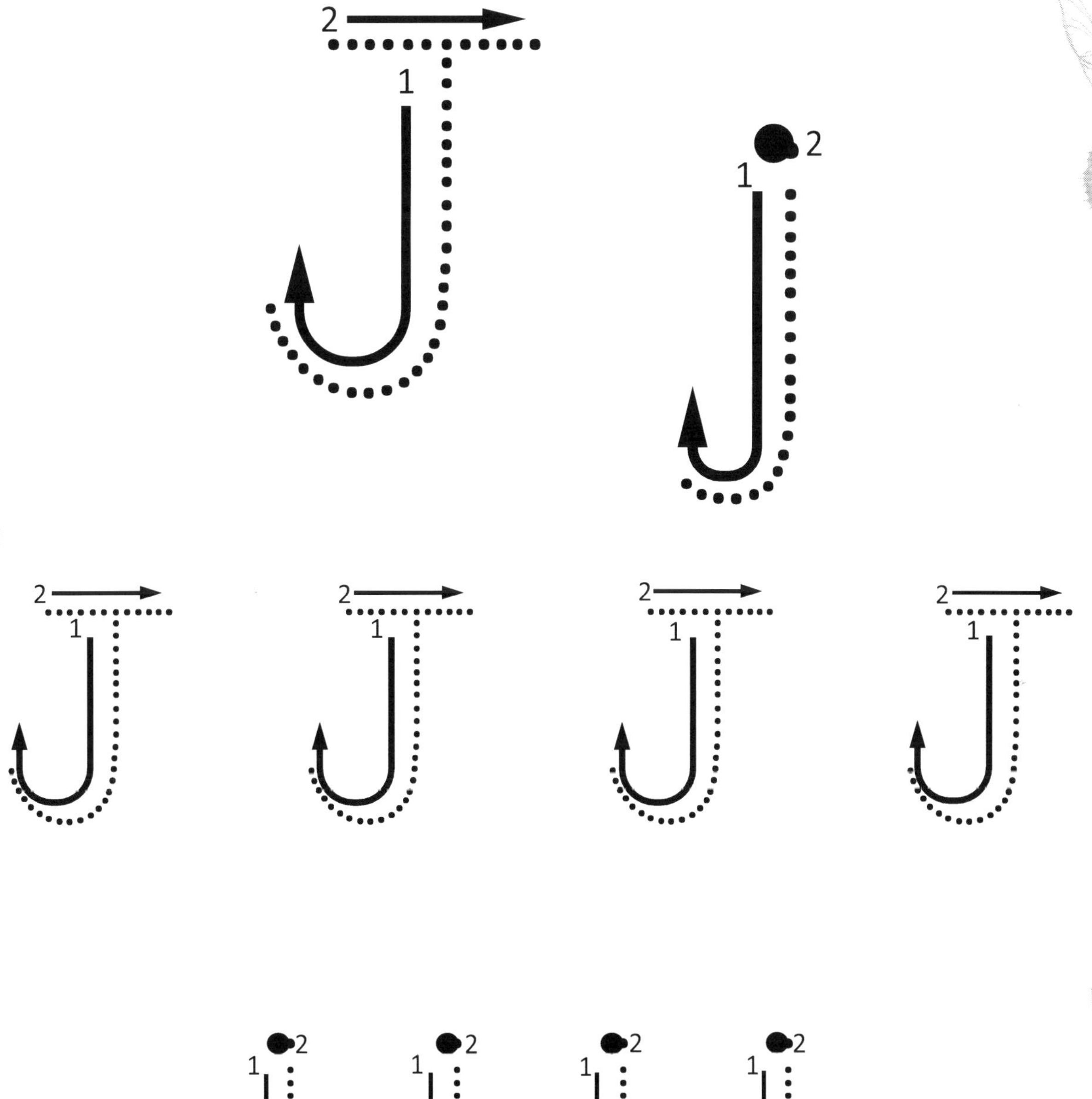

J is for Jump!

Thank You God for Jumping!

Jump

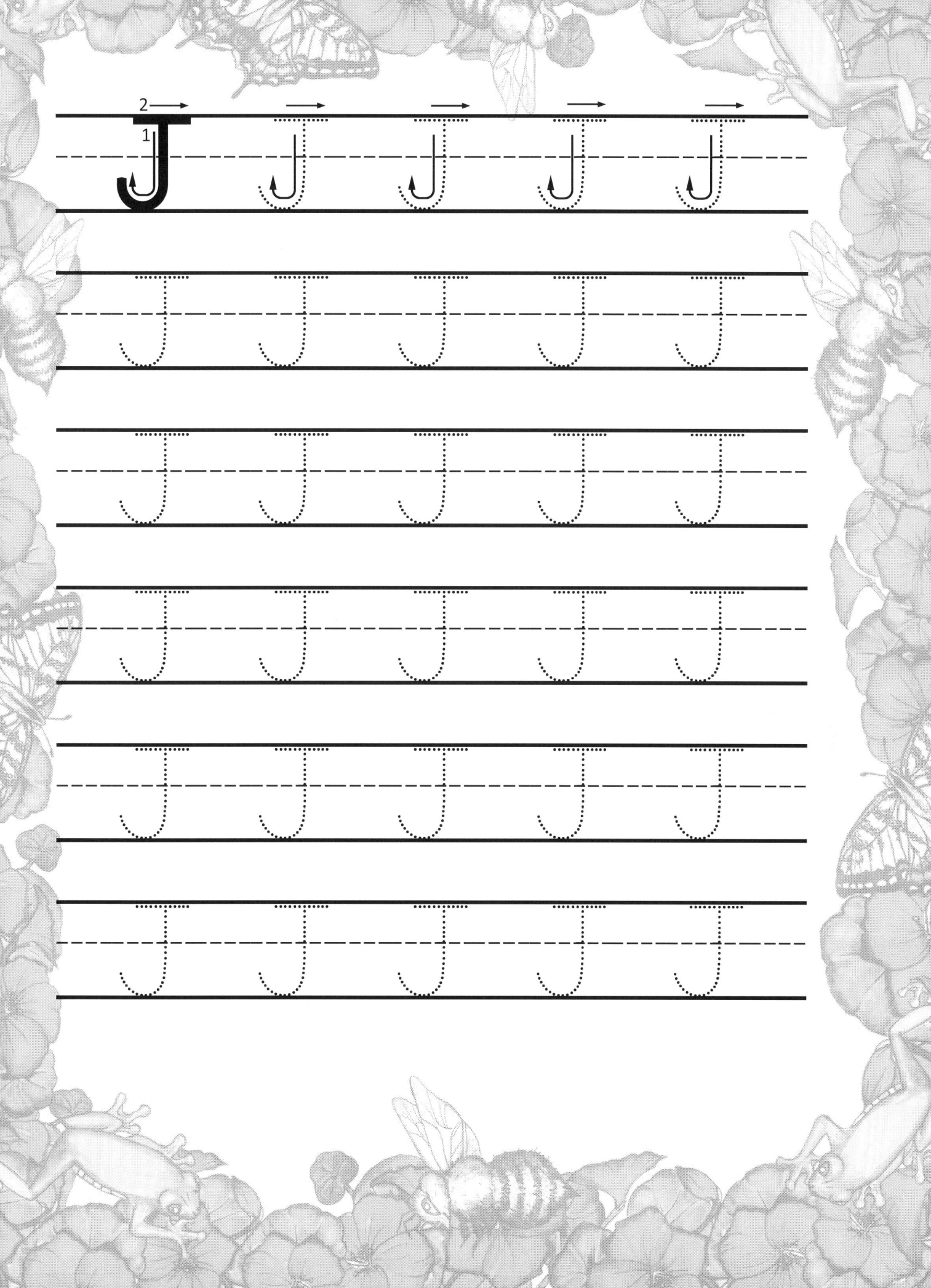

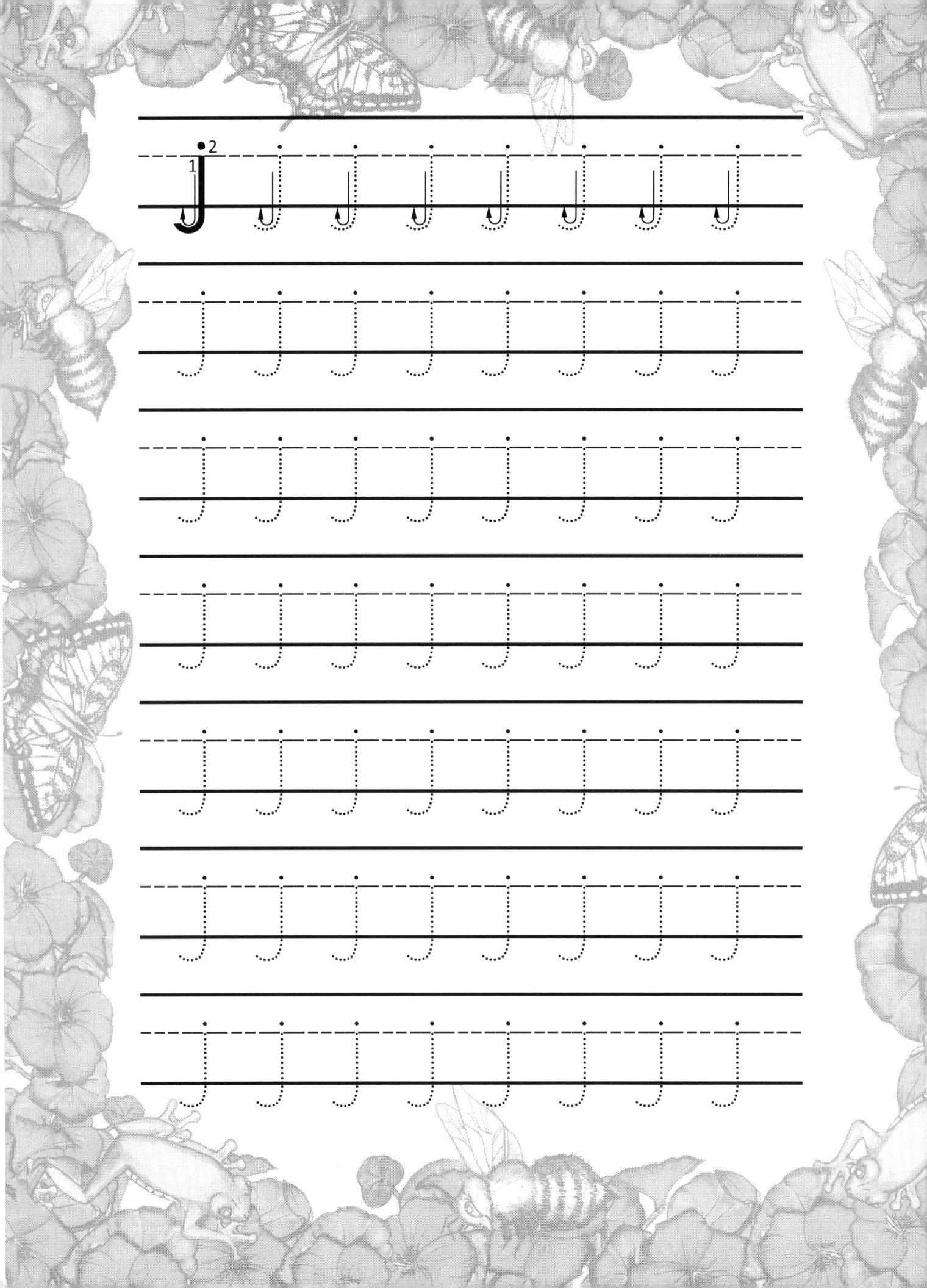

The letter K

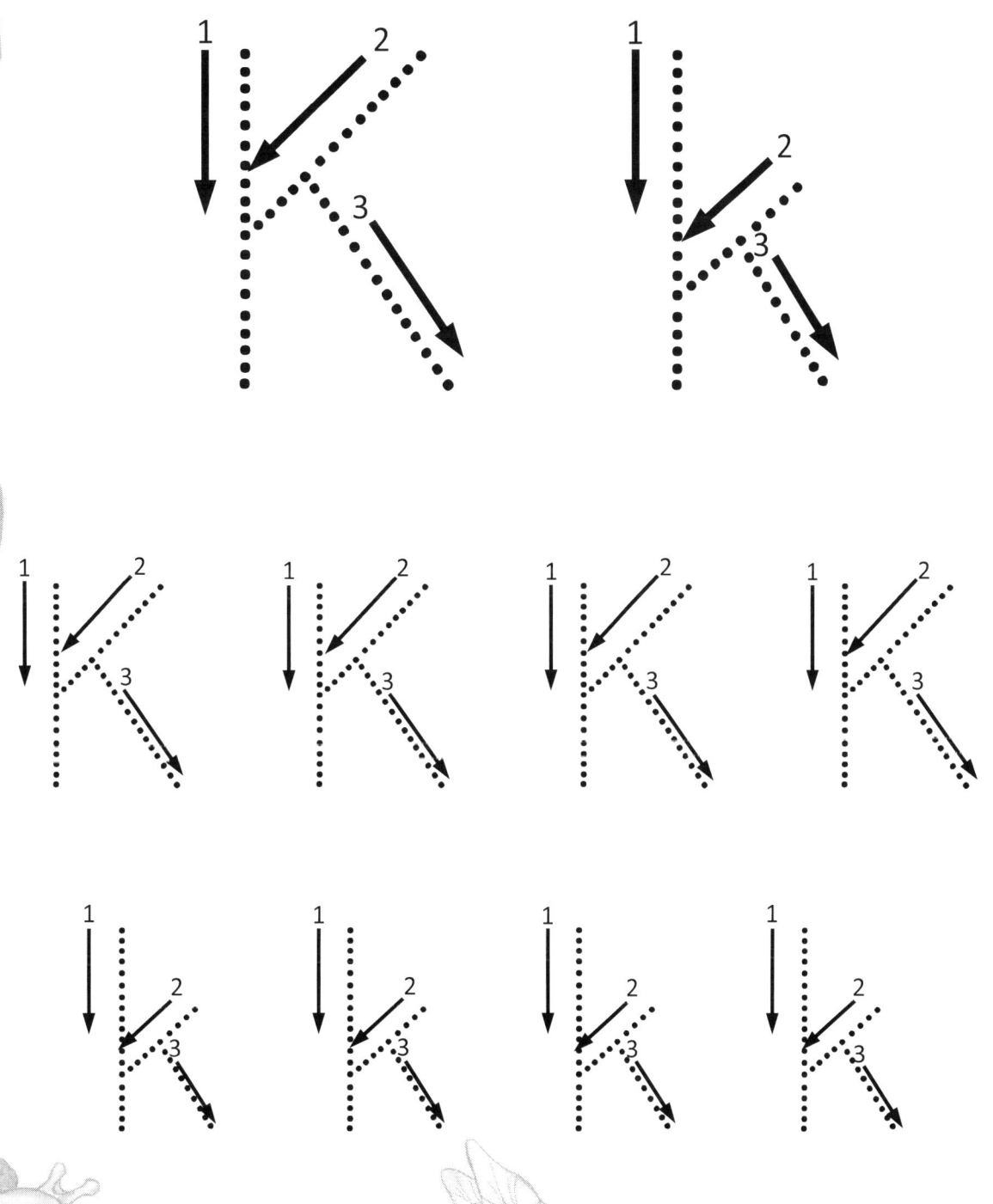

K is for Kingfisher!

Thank You God for Kingfishers!

Kingfisher

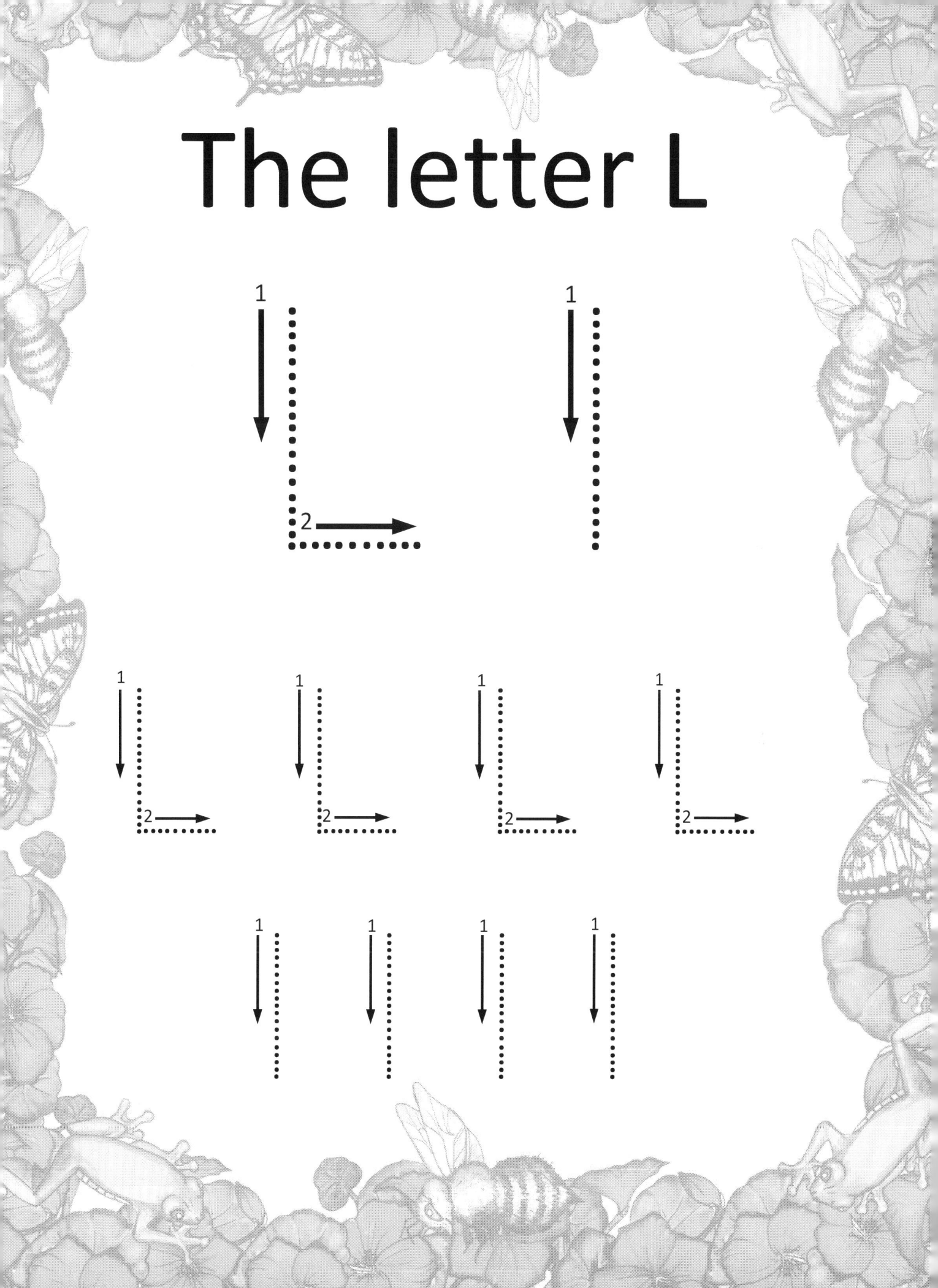

L is Leaf!

Thank You God for Leaves!

Leaf

The letter M

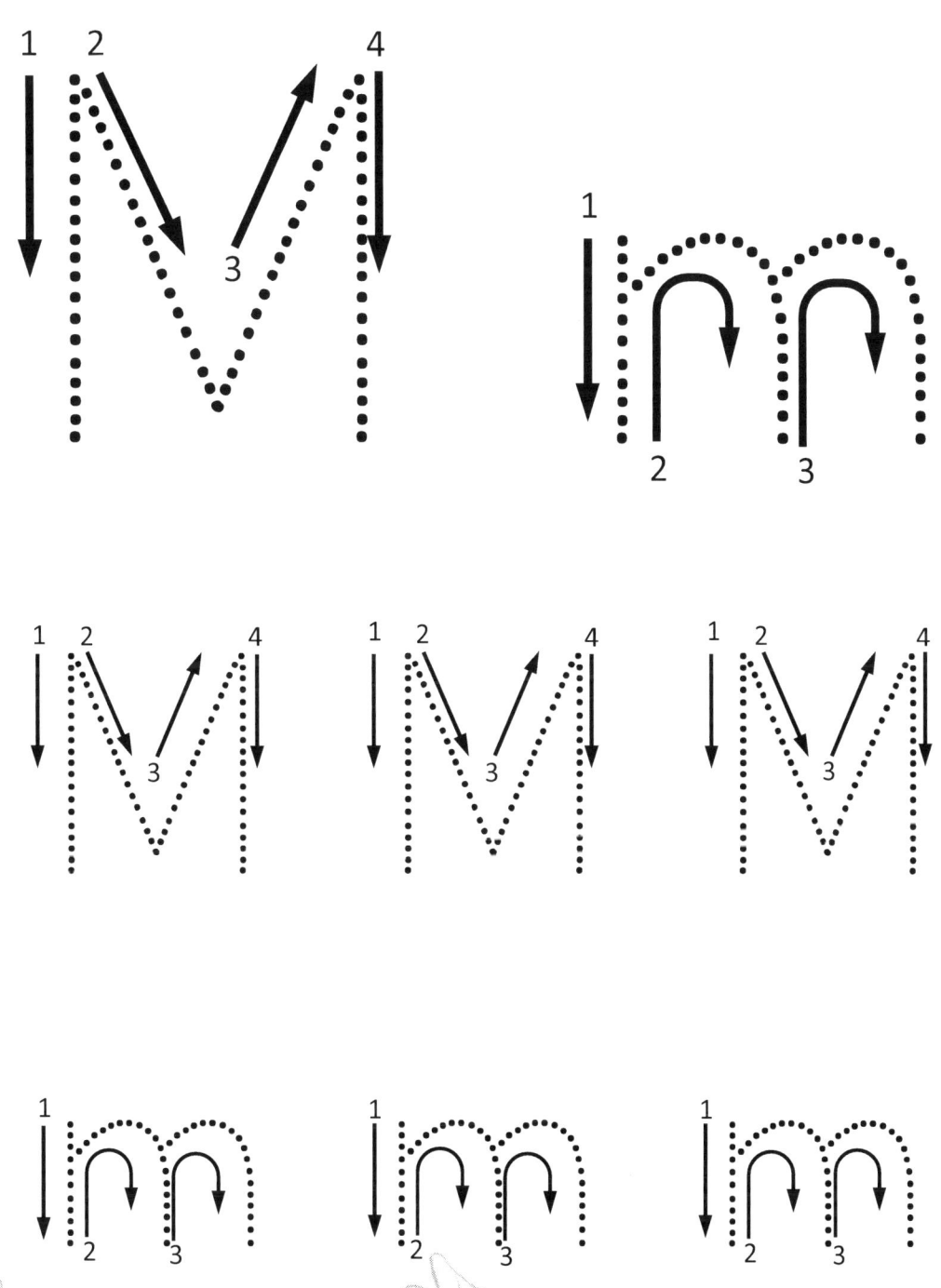

M is for Mouse!

Thank You God for Mice!

Mouse

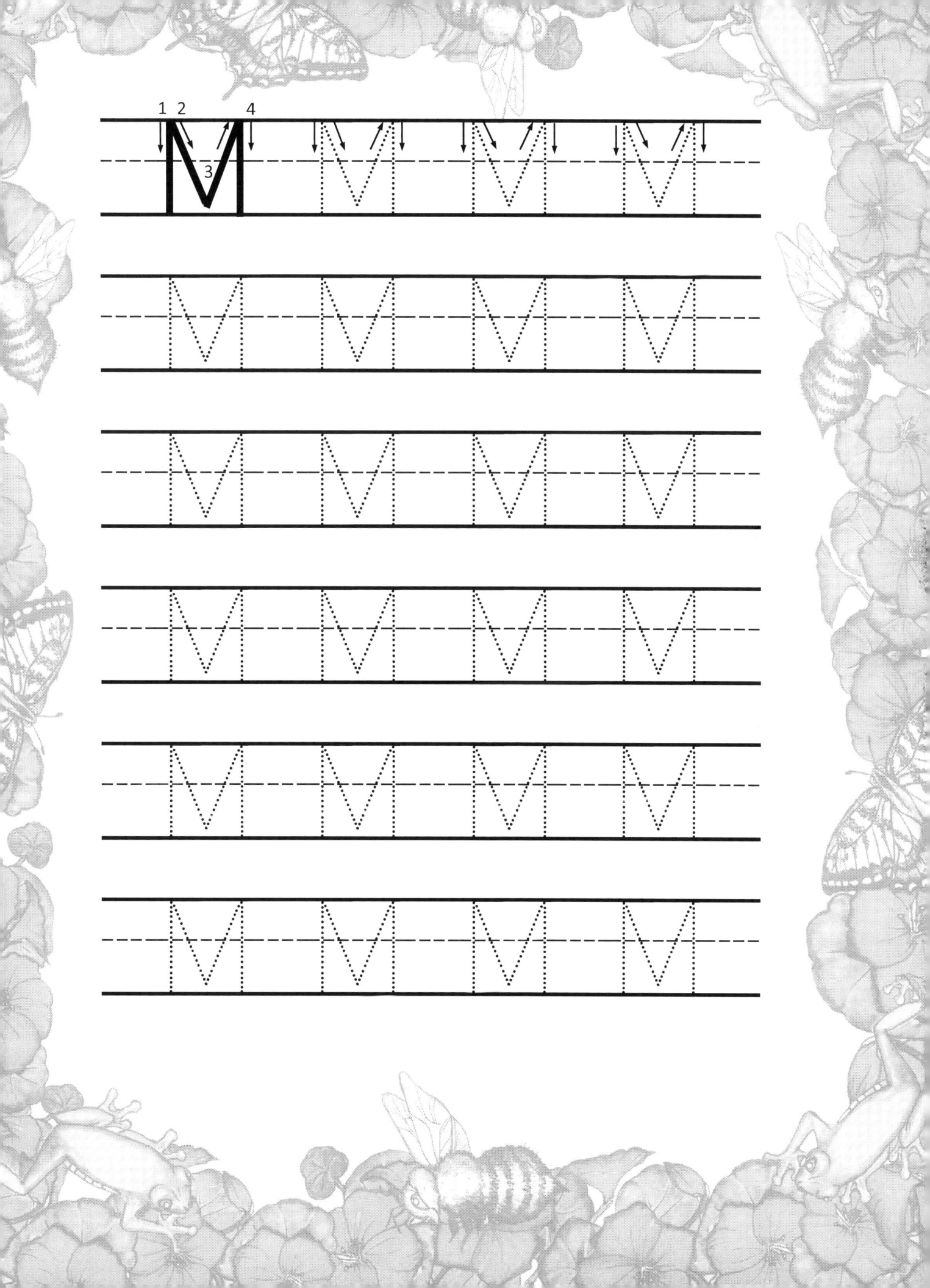

The letter N

N is for Nest!

Thank You God for Nests!

Nest

The letter O

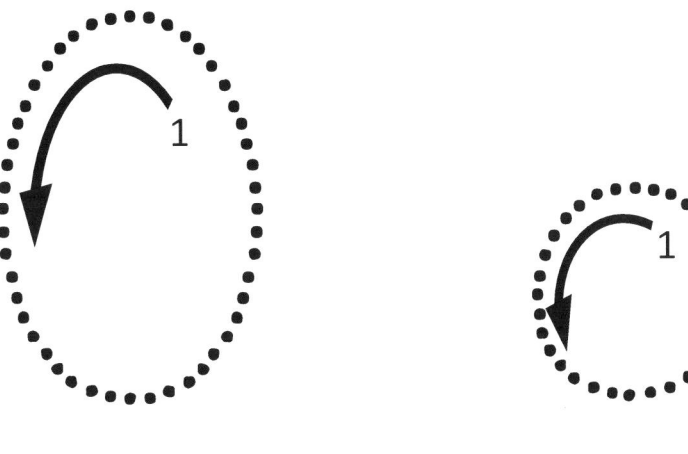
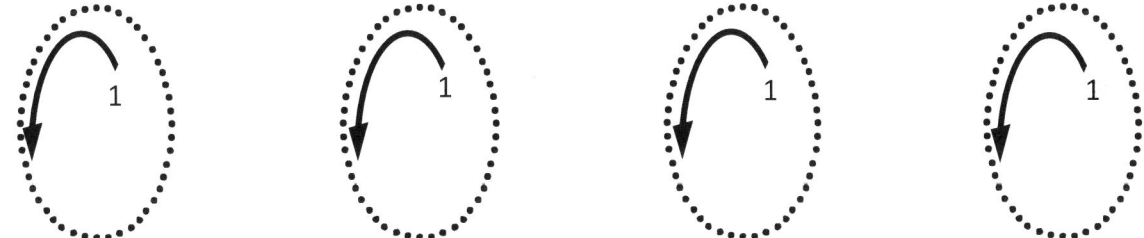

O is for Orange!

Thank You God for Orange butterflies!

Nest

The letter P

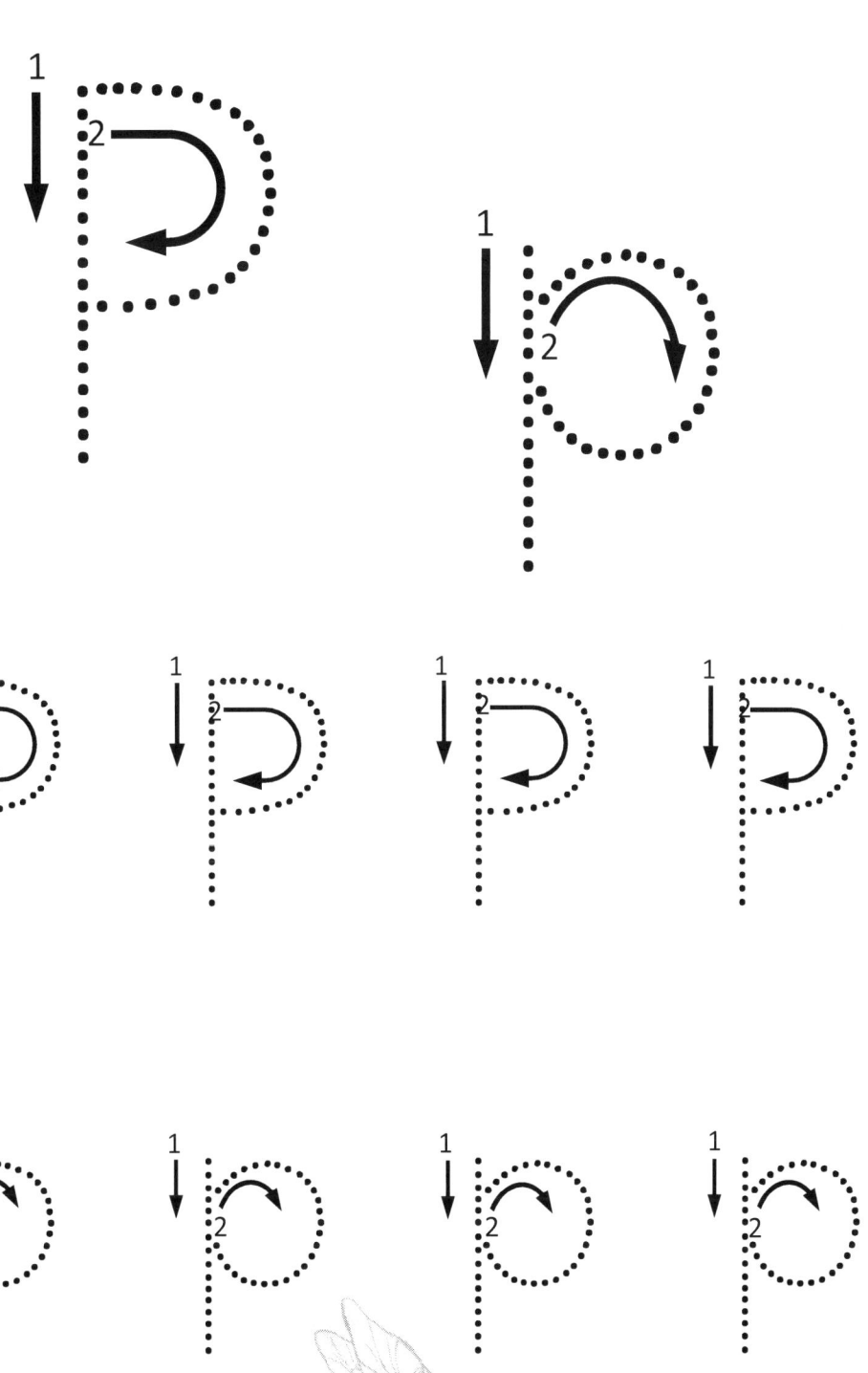

P is for Pumpkin!

Thank You God for Pumpkins!

Pumpkin

p

The letter Q

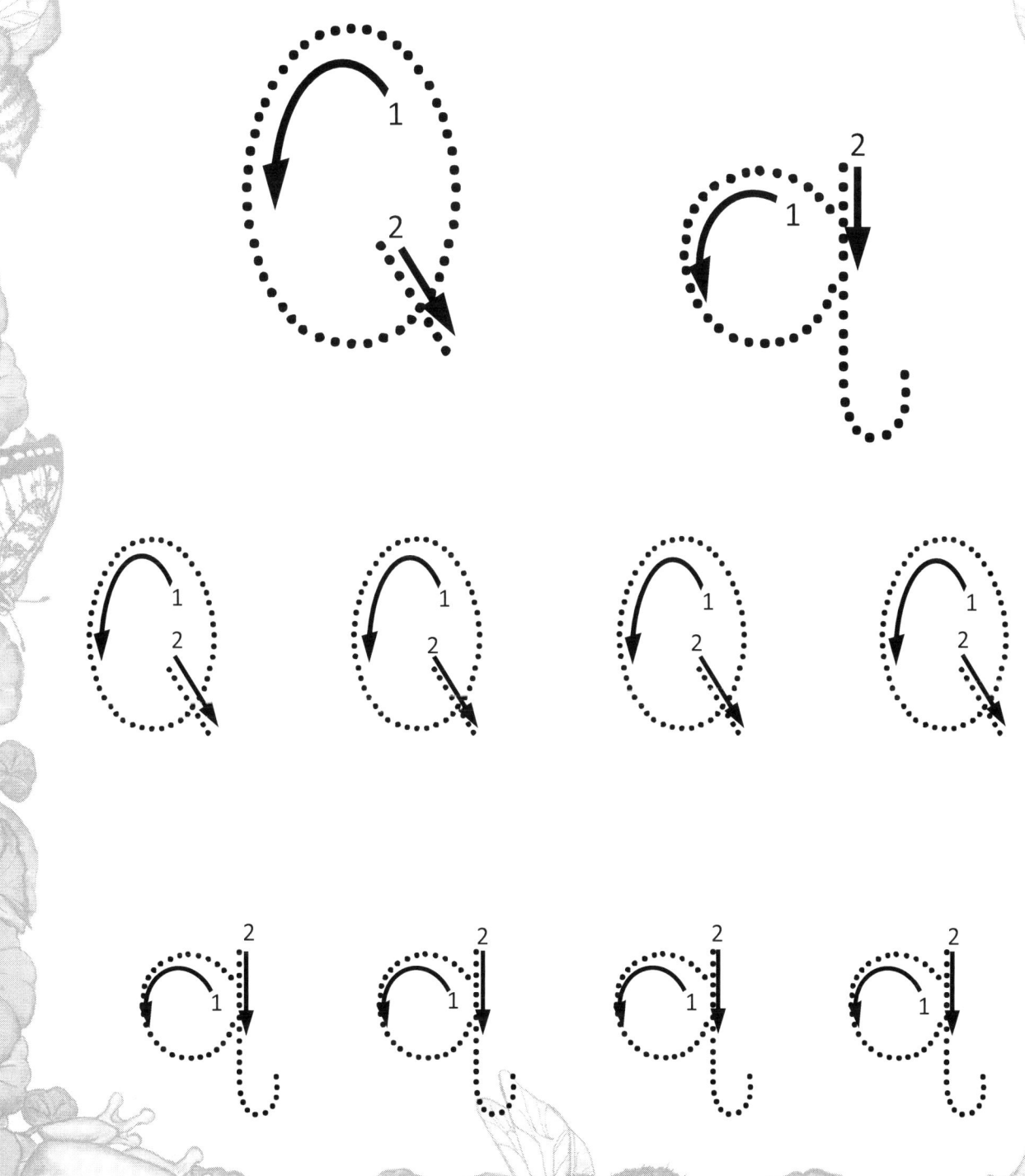

Q is for Quack!

Thank You God for Quacking ducks!

The letter R

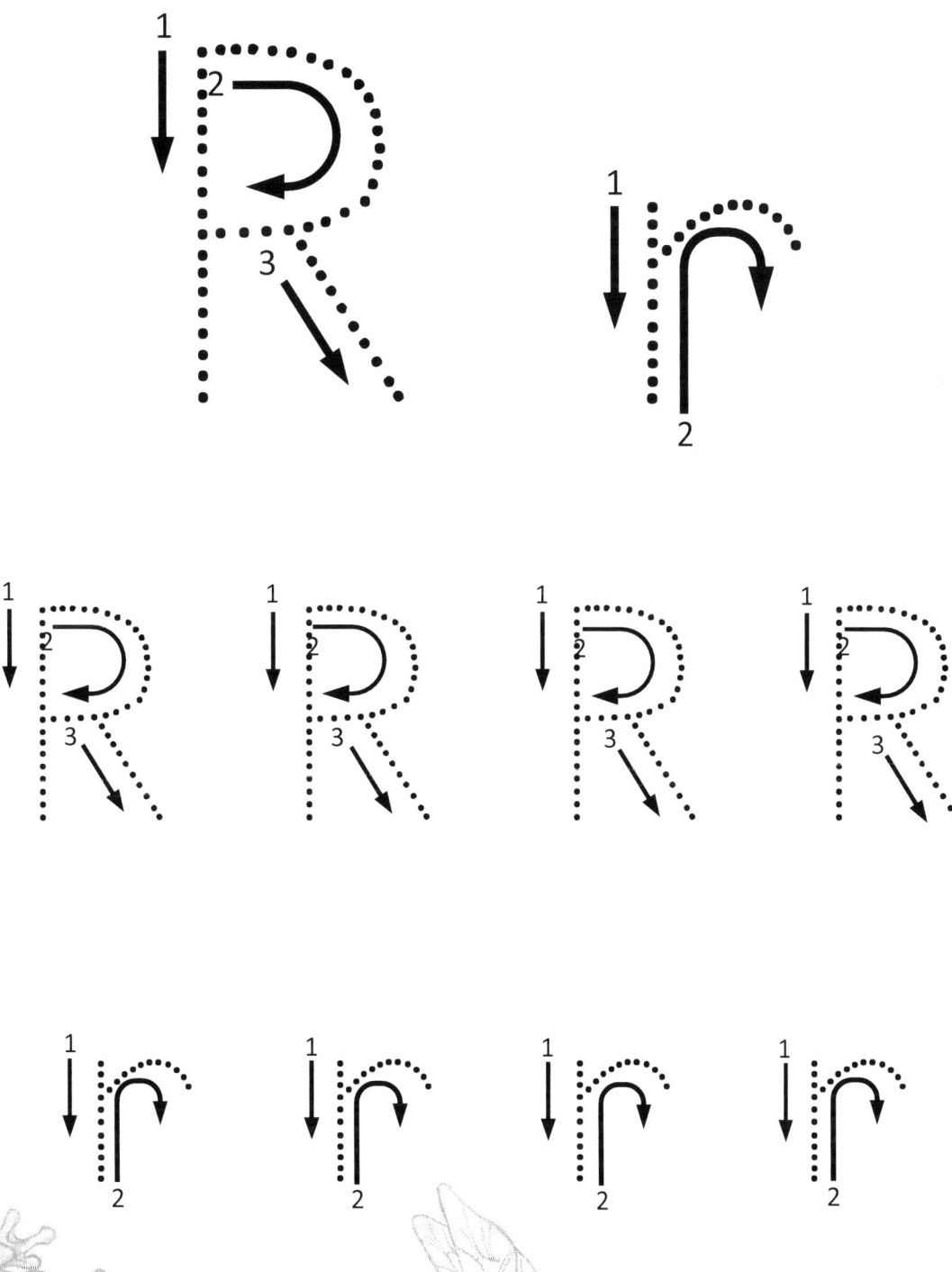

R is for Rabbit!

Thank You God for Rabbits!

Rabbit

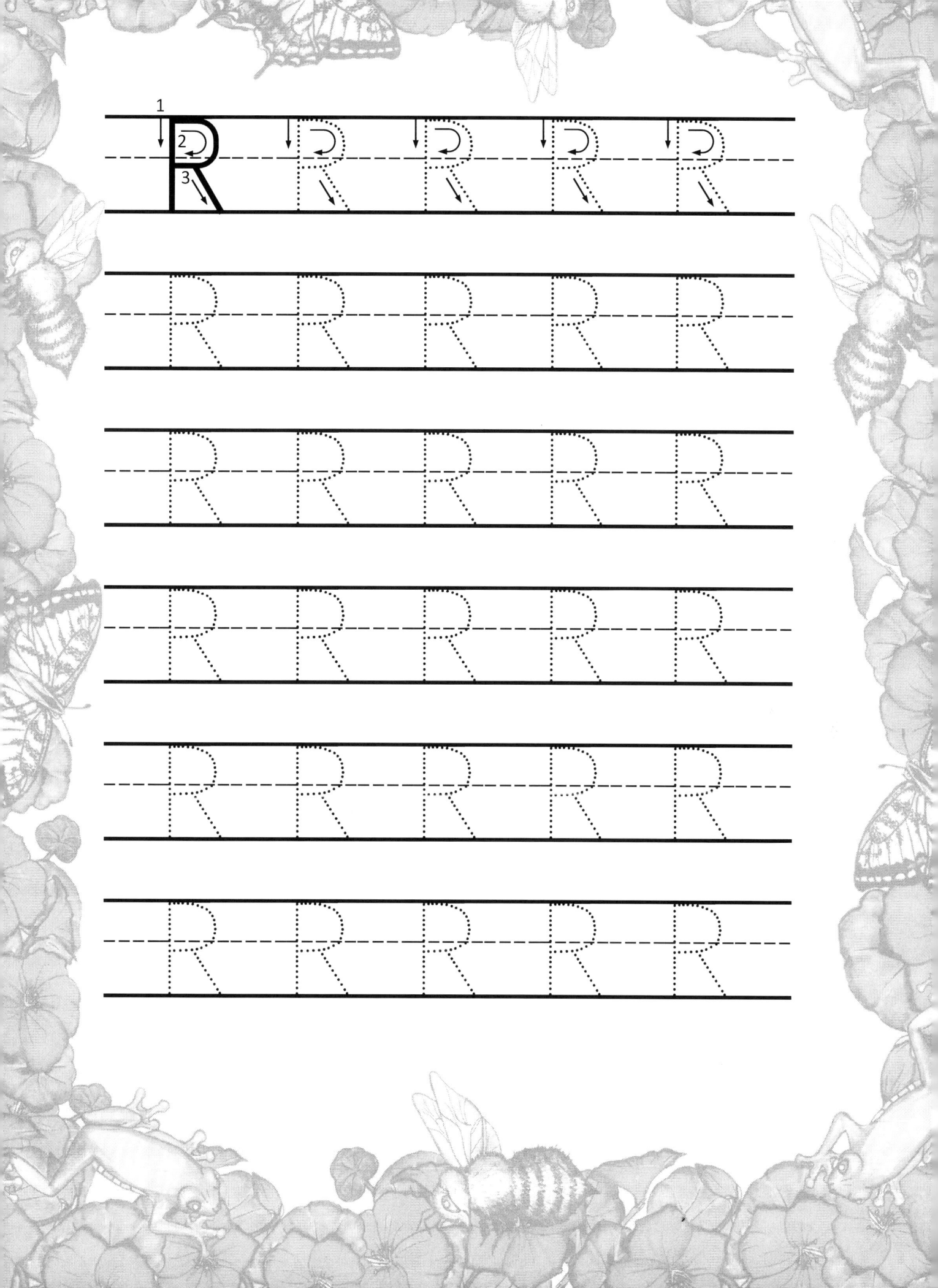

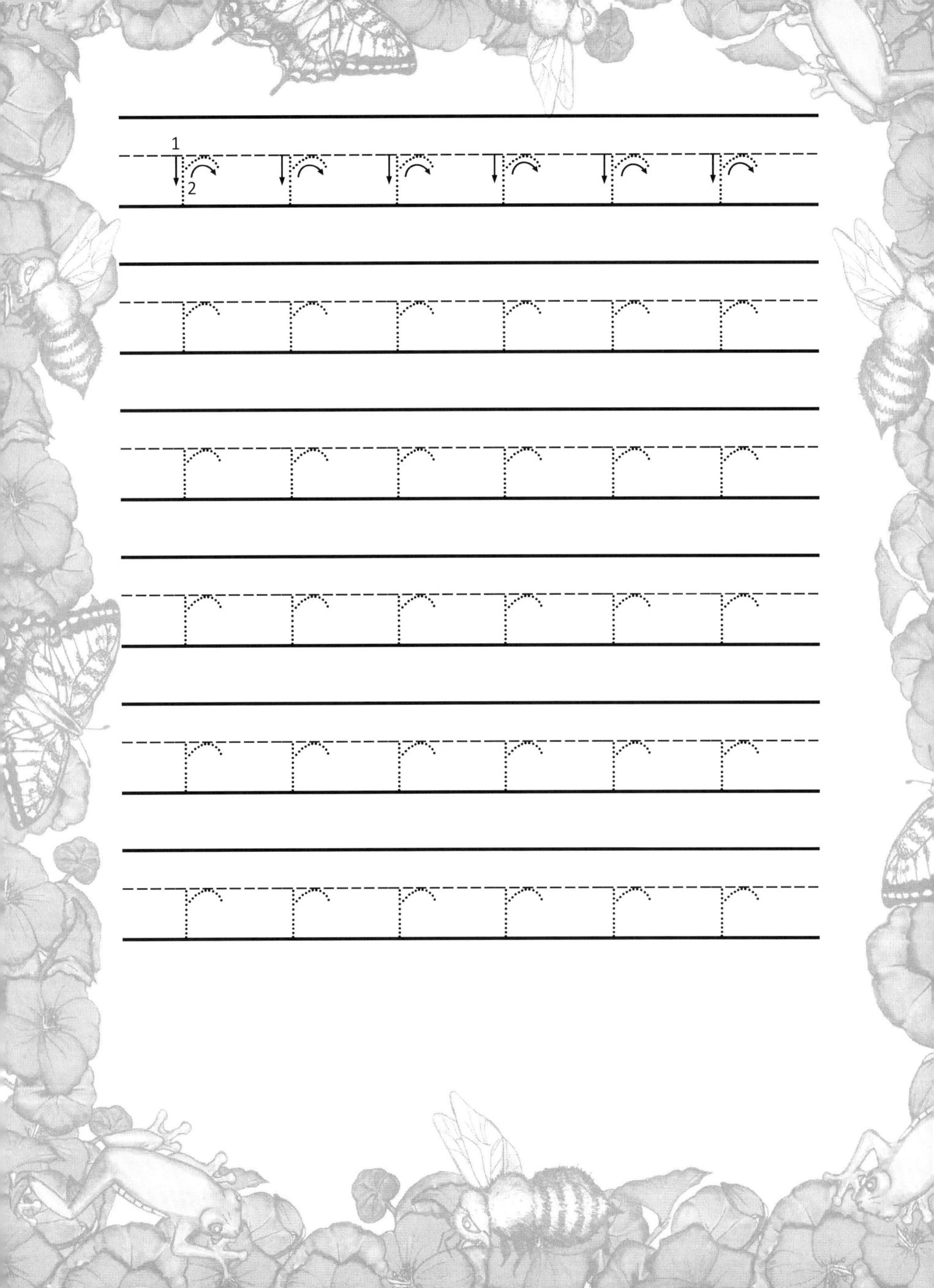

The letter S

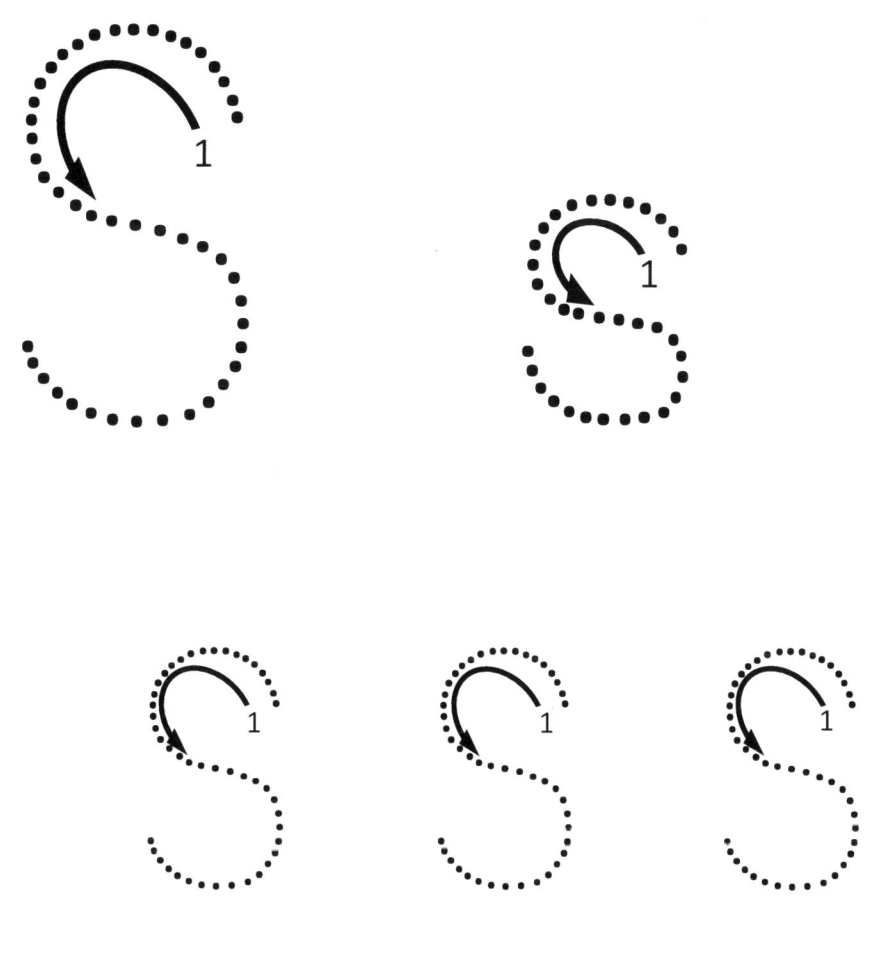

S is for Sunflower!

Thank You God for Sunflowers!

Sunflower

The letter T

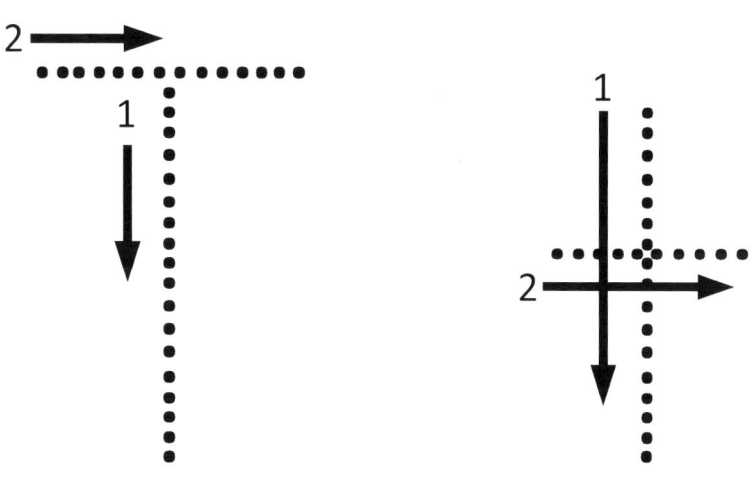
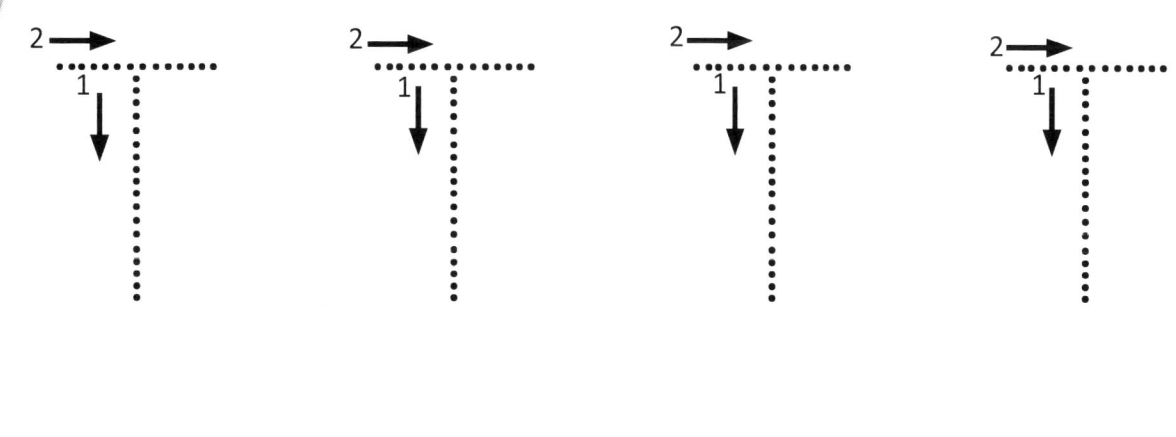
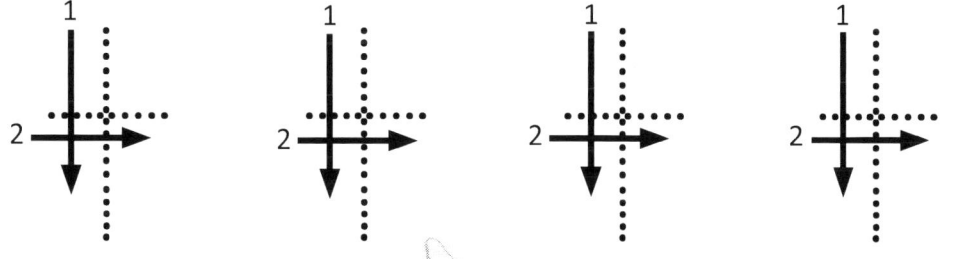

T is for Tree!

Thank You God for Trees!

Sunflower

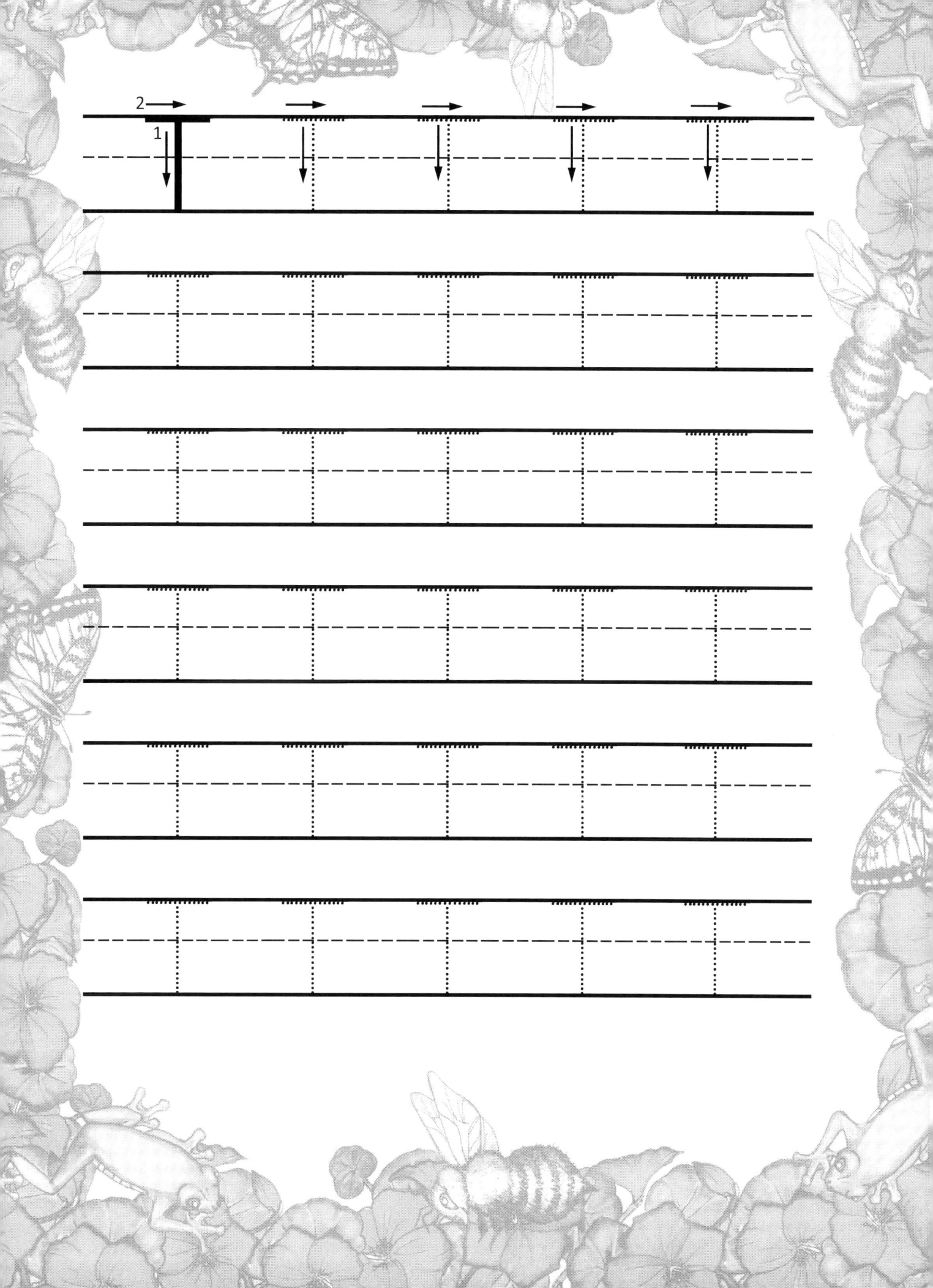

The letter U

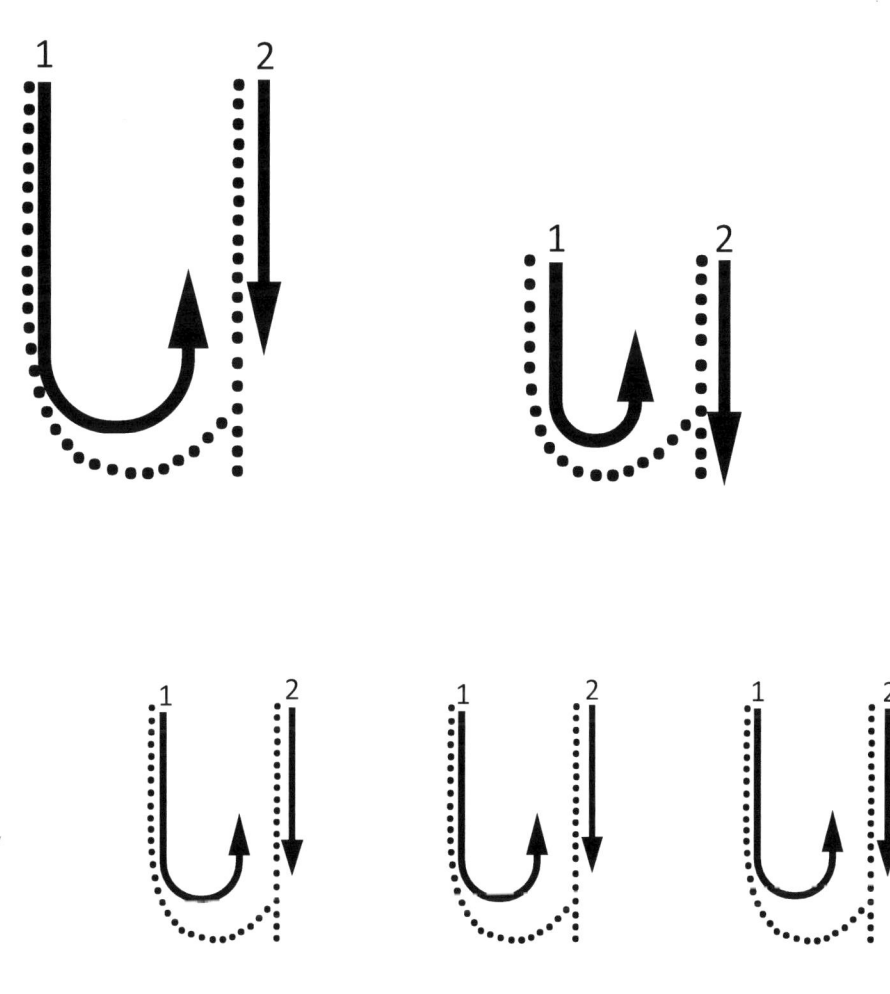

U is for Universe!
Thank You God for the great big Universe!

Universe

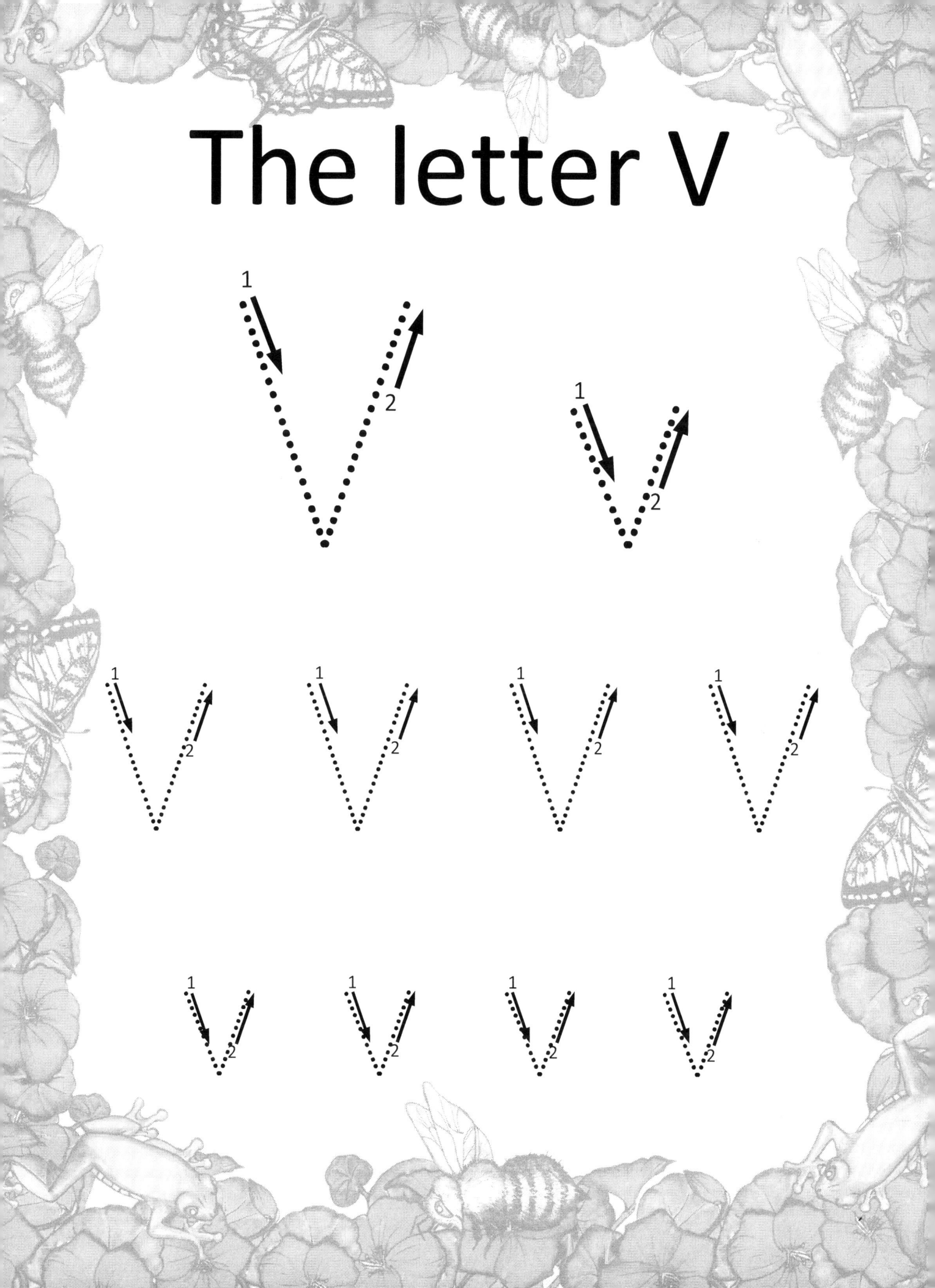

V is for Vegetable!
Thank You God for delicious Vegetables!

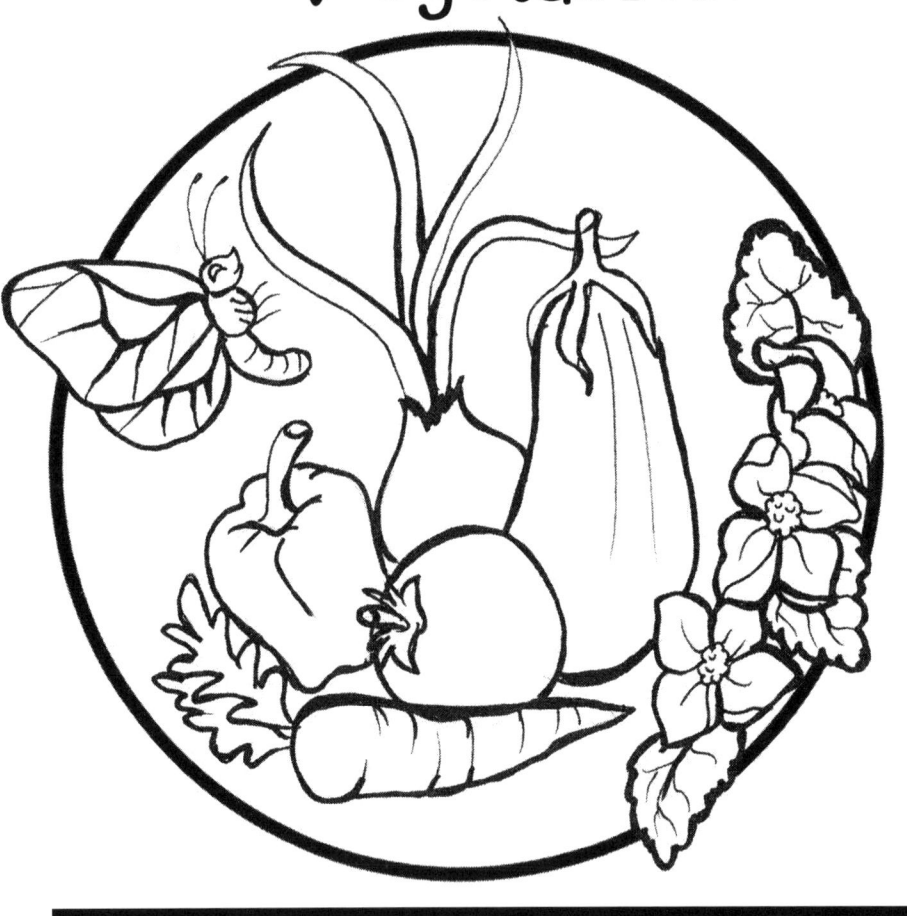

Vegetable

The letter W

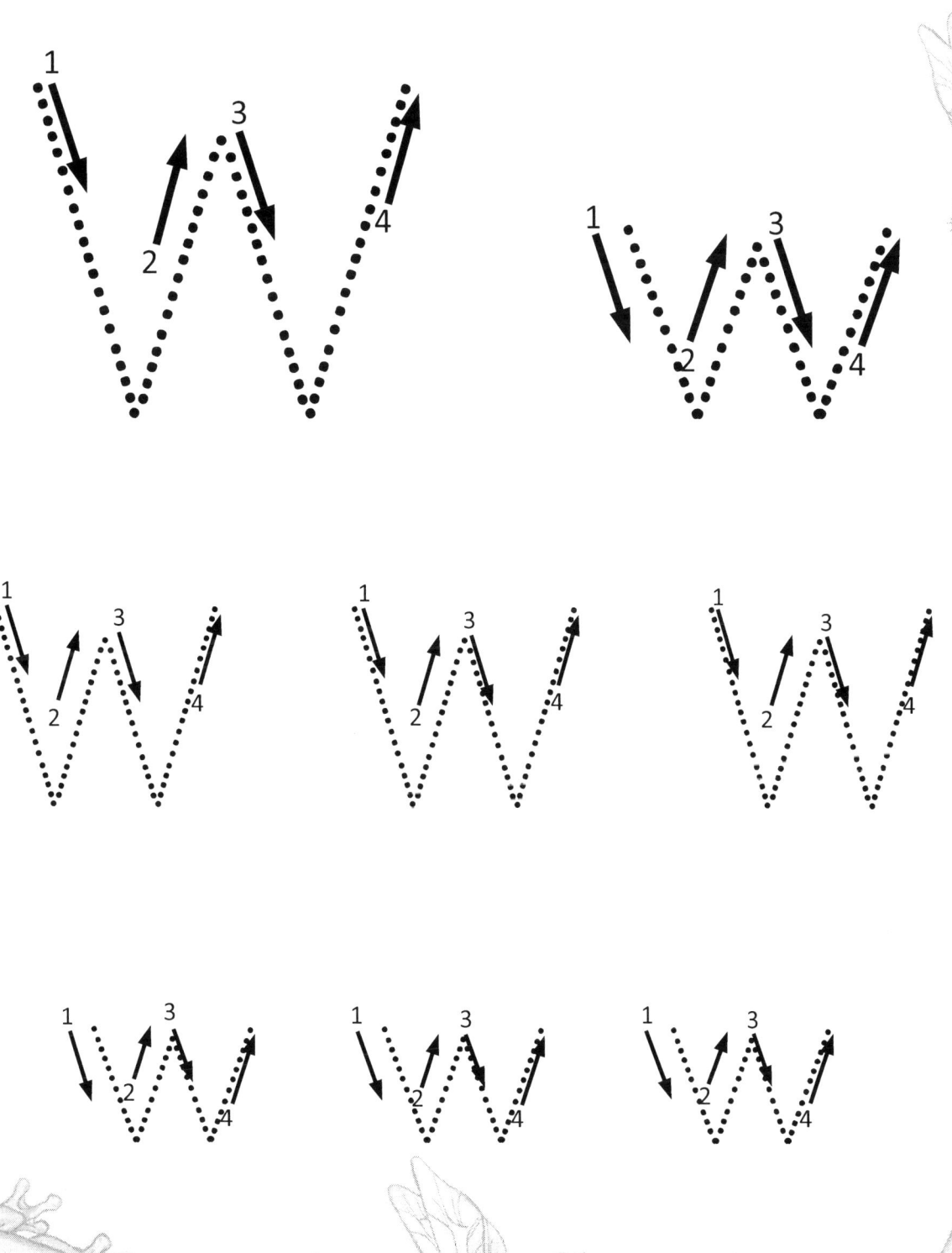

W is for Wing!
Thank You God for the flying animals' Wings!

Wing

The letter X

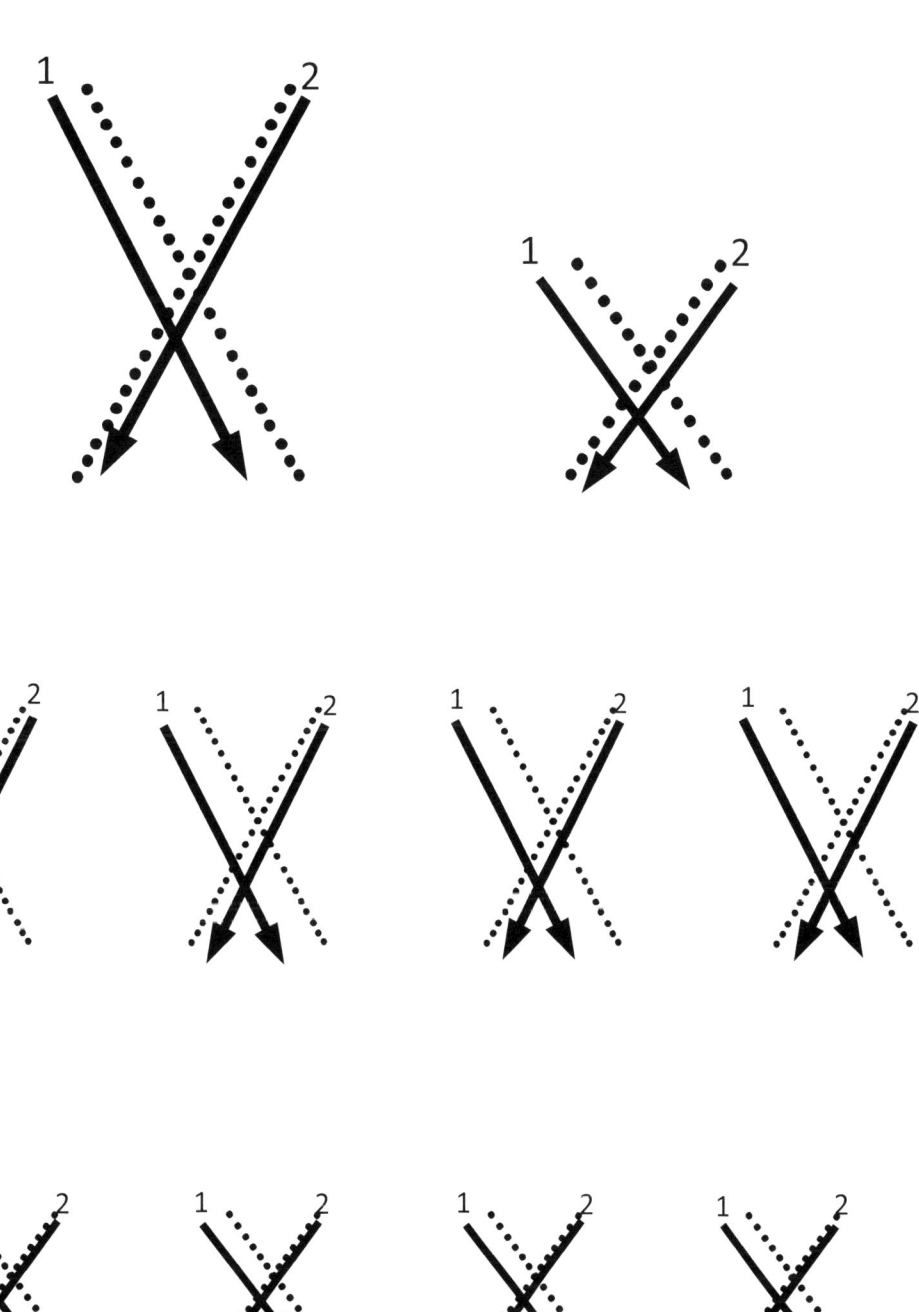

X is for X-ray Fish!

Thank You God for X-ray fish!

X-ray Fish

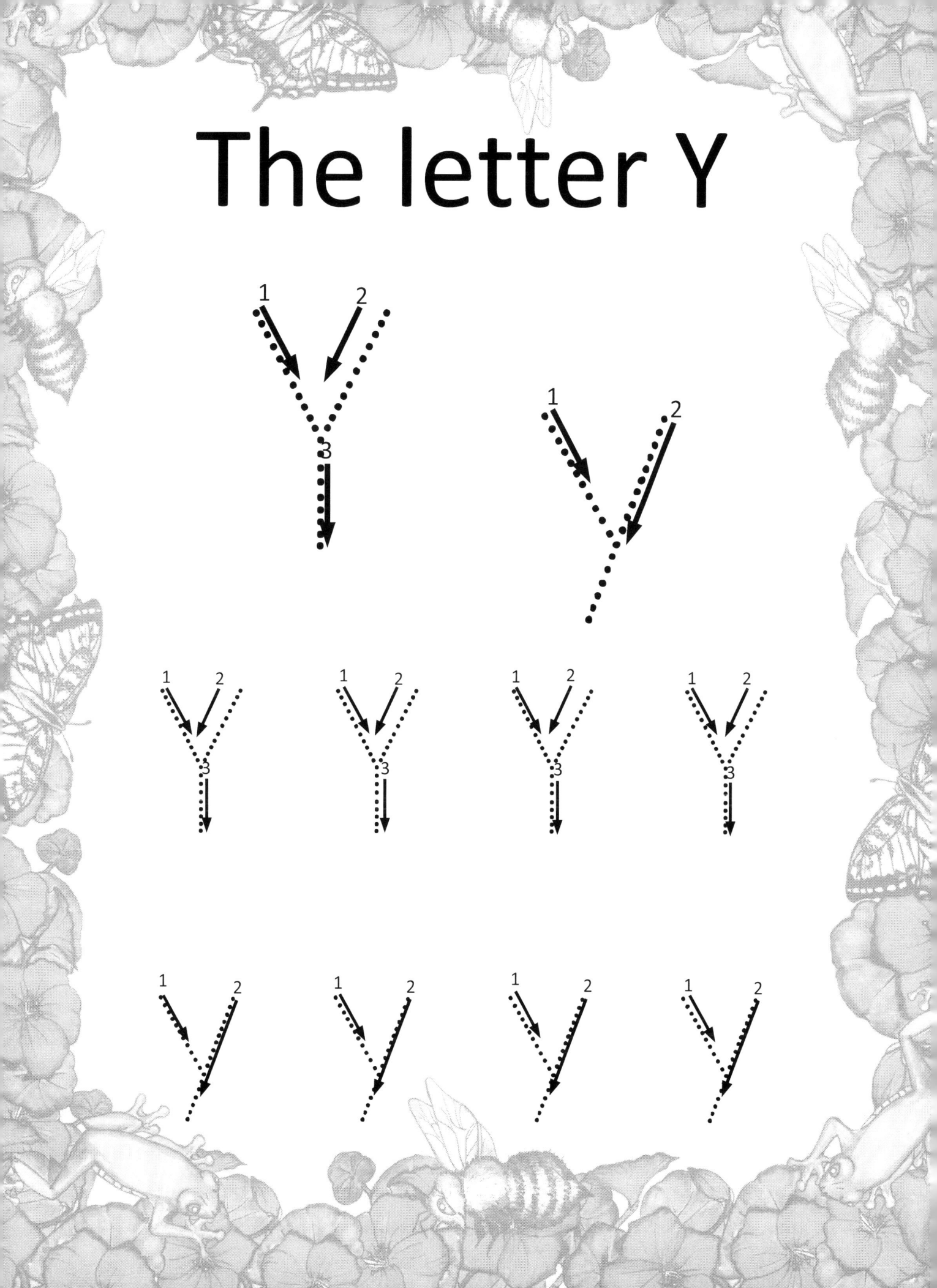

Y is for Yellow!
Thank You God for lovely
Yellow butterflies!

Yellow

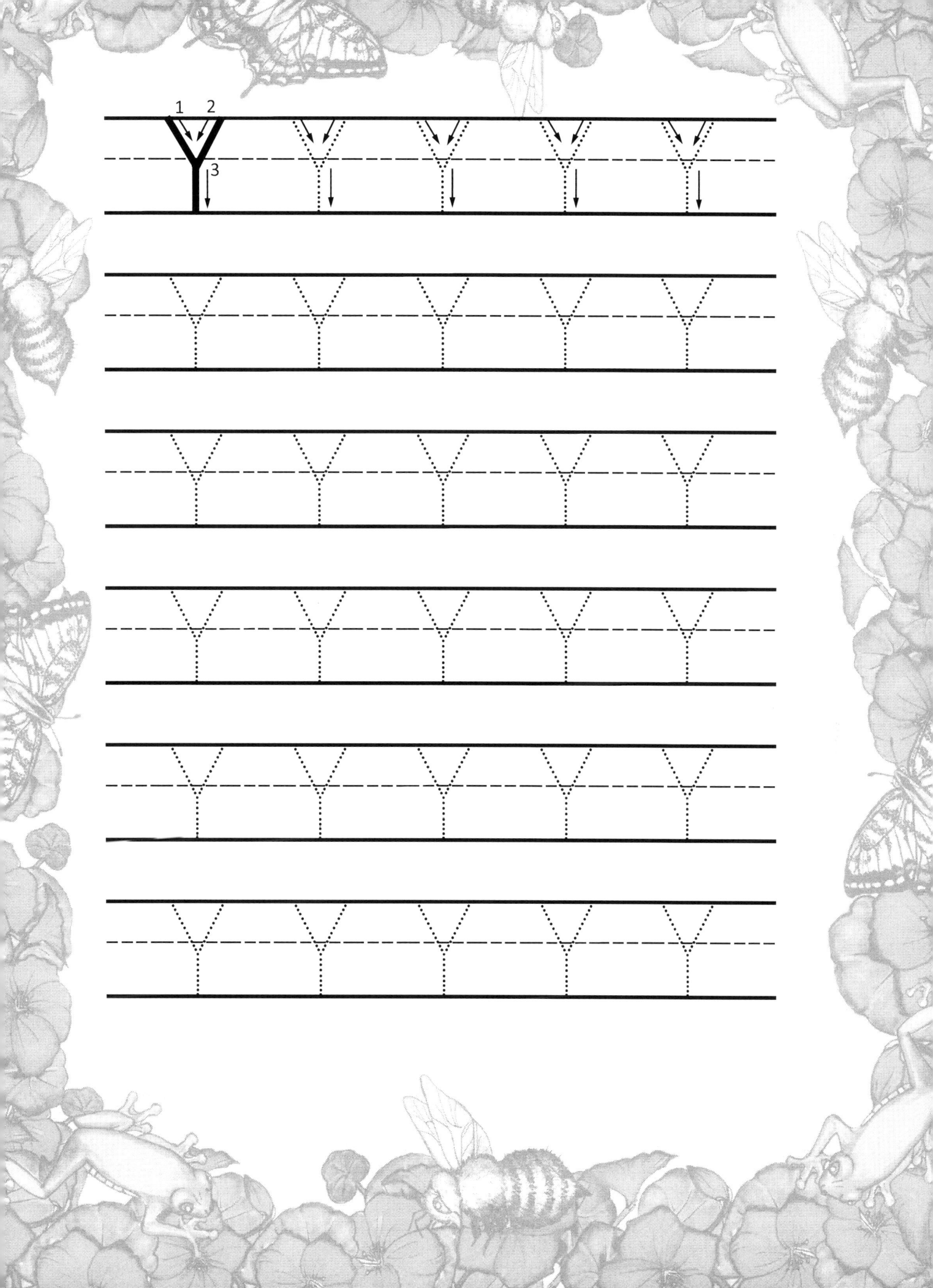

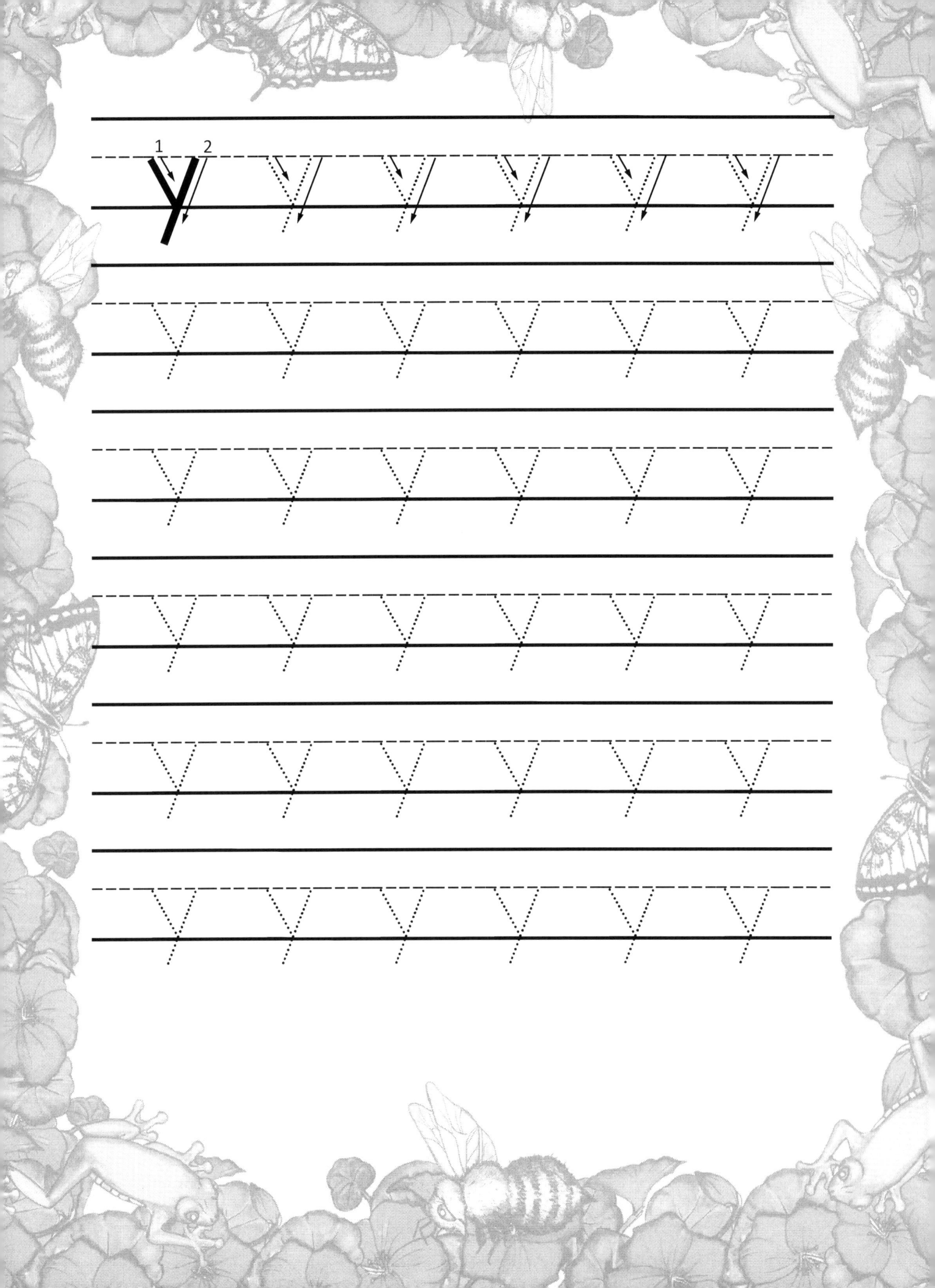

The letter Z

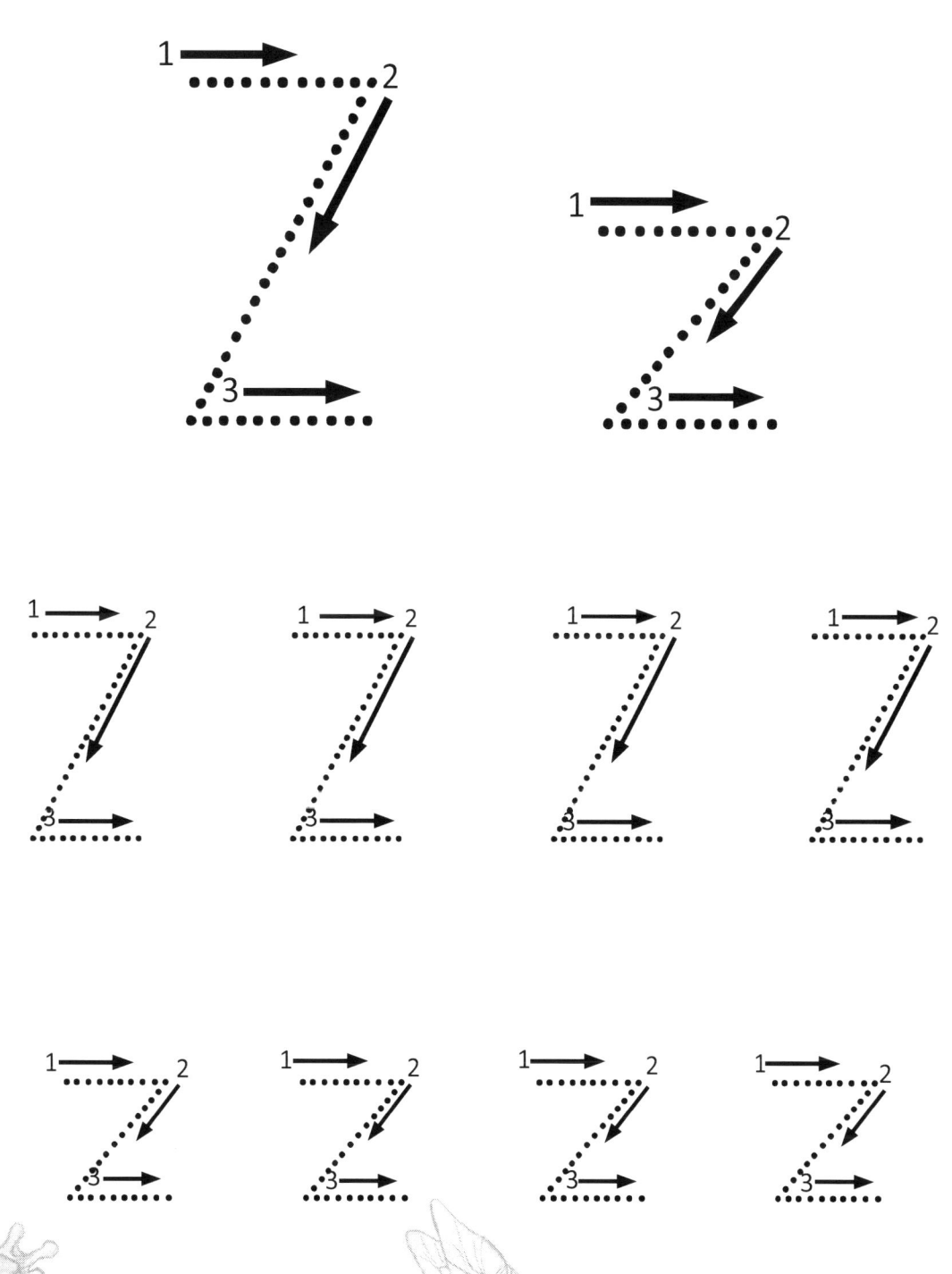

Z is for Zinnia!

Thank You God for Zinnia Flowers!

Zinnia

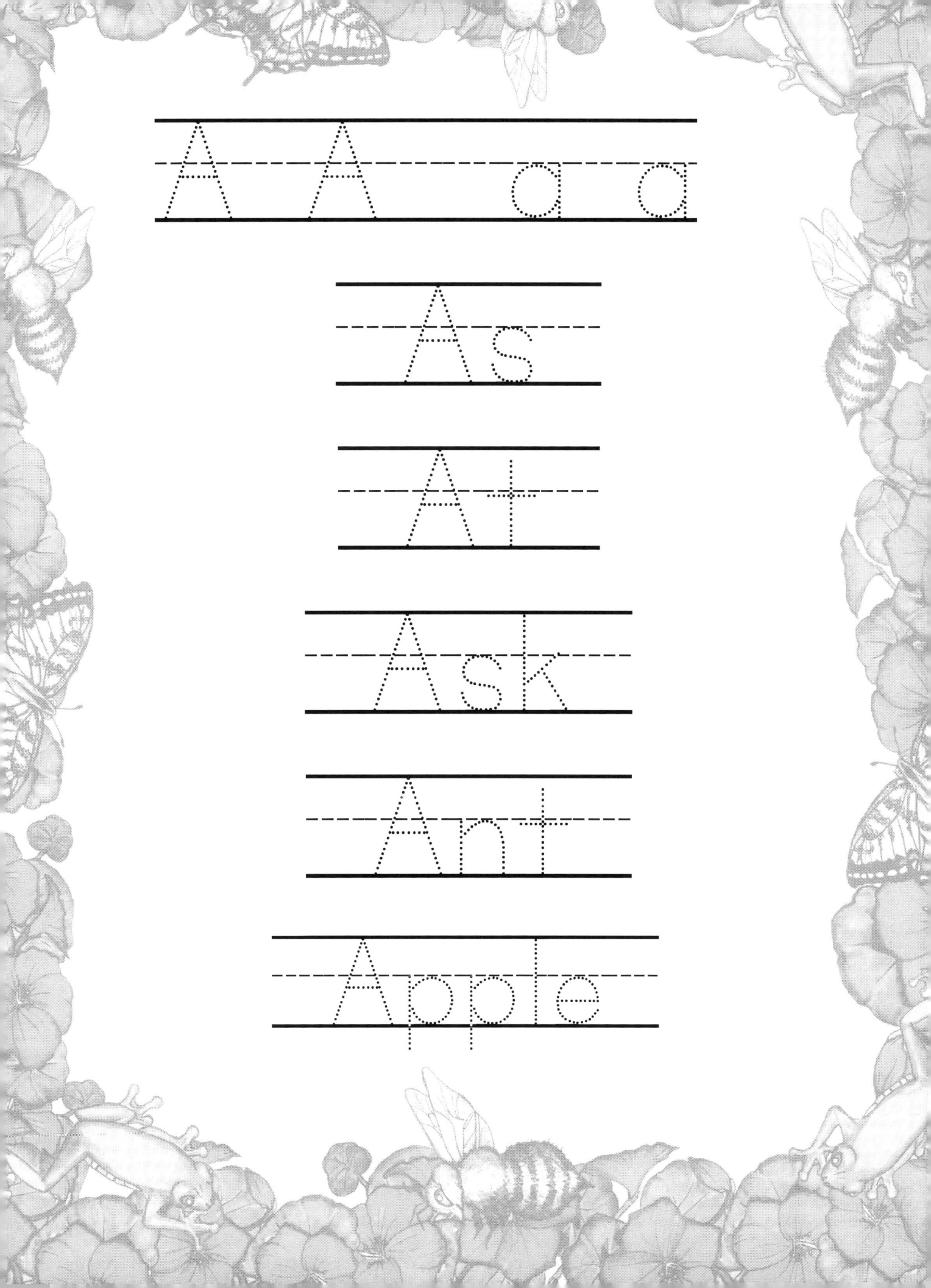

B B b b

Bee

Blue

Bird

Baby

Bible

G G g g

Go

God

Give

Good

Green

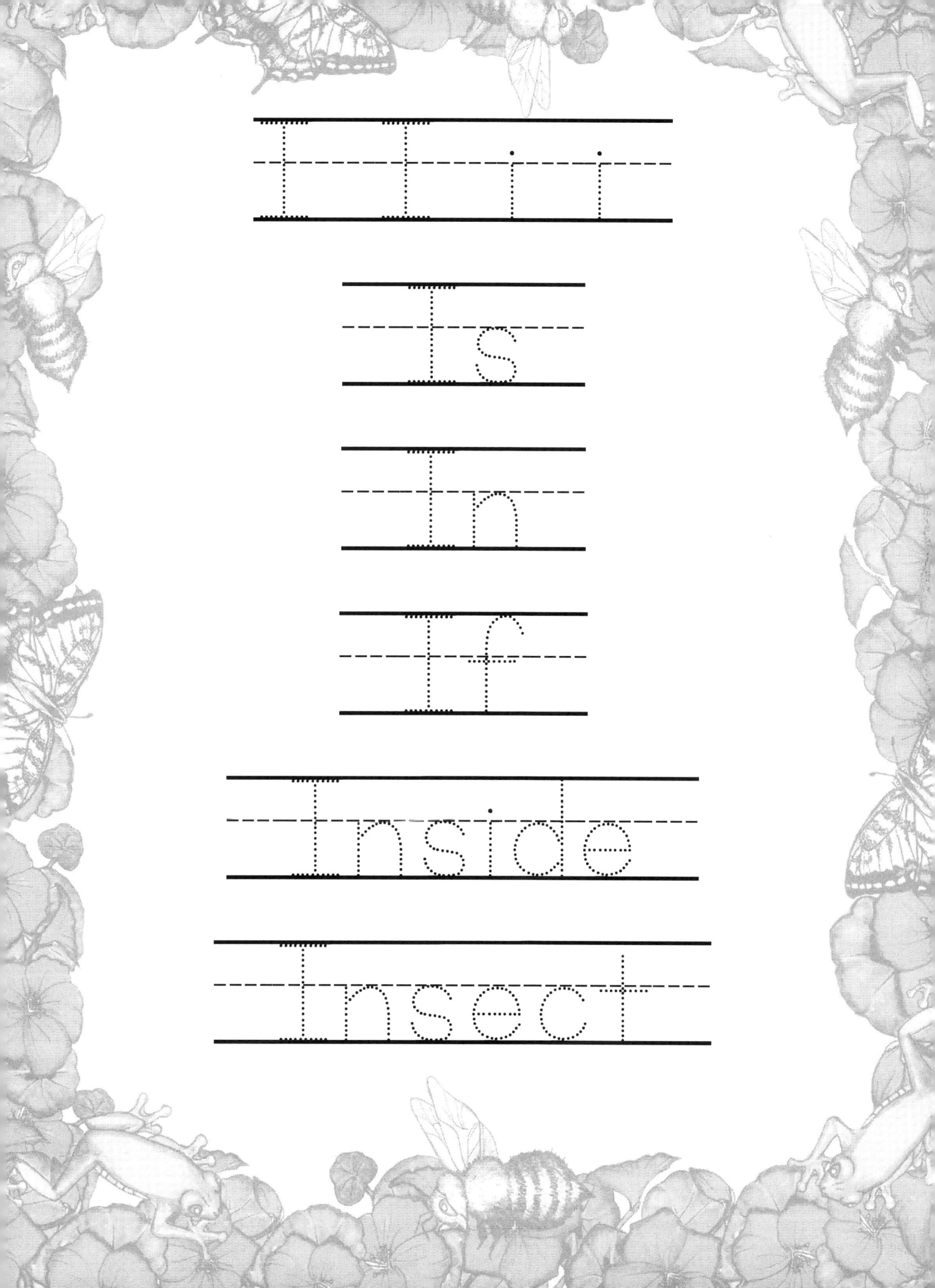

K K K k

Kid

Key

King

Kind

Kingfisher

N N n n

No

New

Nest

Nice

Nine

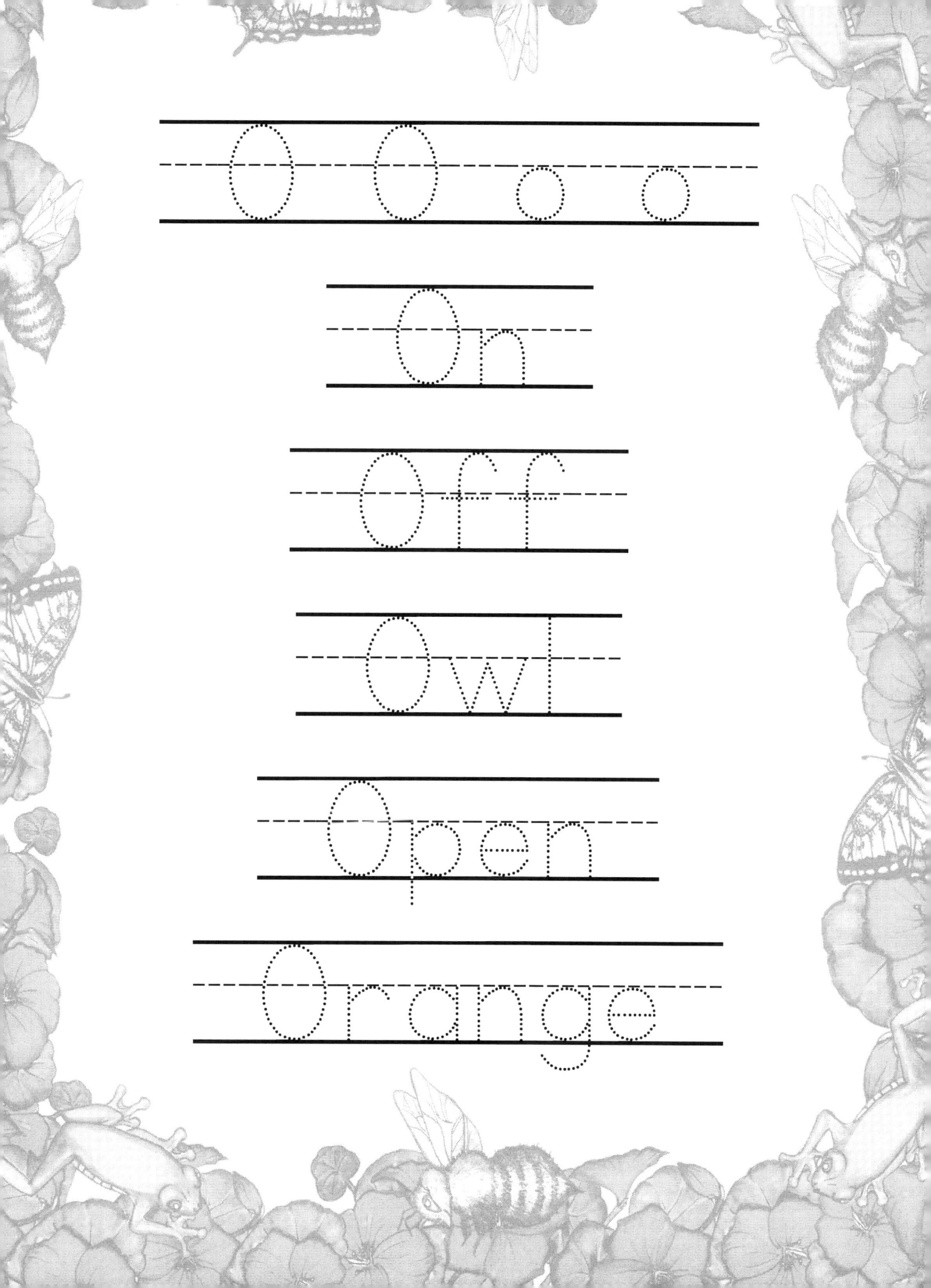

P p p p

Pure

Pond

Place

Perfect

Pumpkin

Q Q q q

Quick

Queen

Quest

Quack

Question

R R R r r r

Red

Rose

Right

Robin

Rabbit

S S s s

So

Sun

Son

Soft

Sunflower

U U u u

Up

Unite

Uplift

Unique

Universe

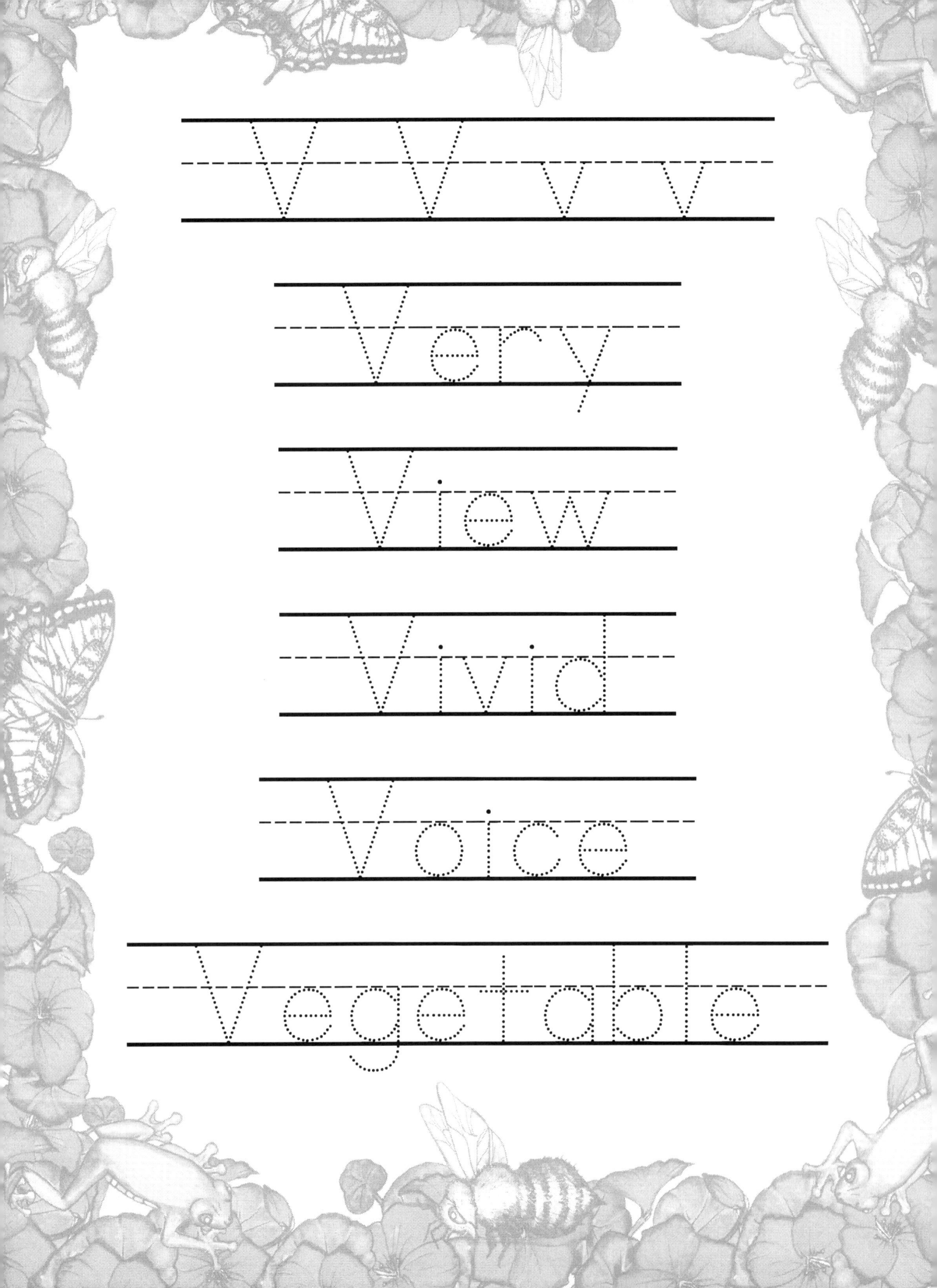

W W w w

we

well

wolf

wing

water

Y Y y y

Yes

You

Yam

Youth

Yellow

Zz Zz Zz

Zoo

Zero

Zoom

Zinnia

Zucchini

Practice Pages

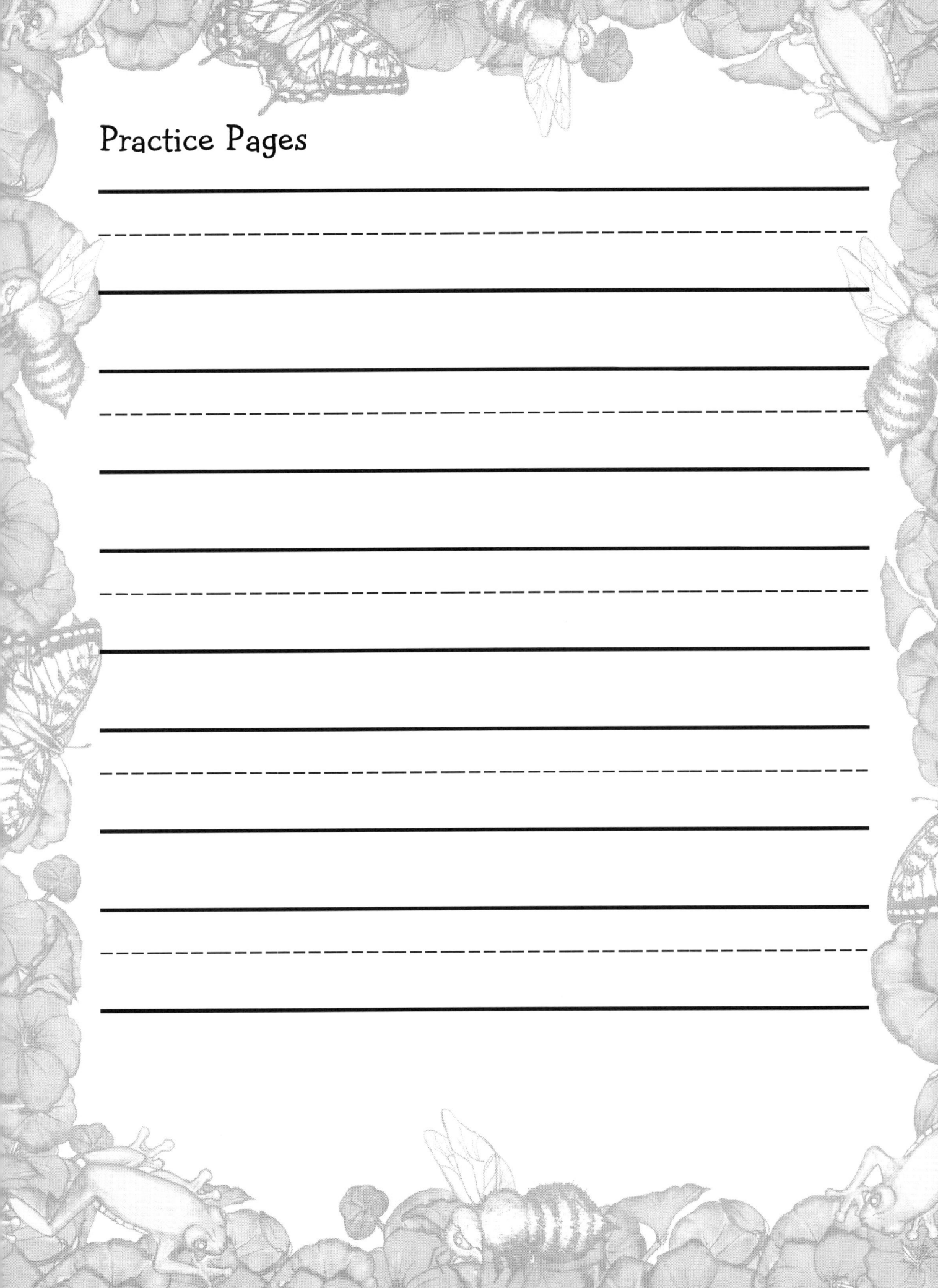
Practice Pages

Practice Pages

Practice Pages

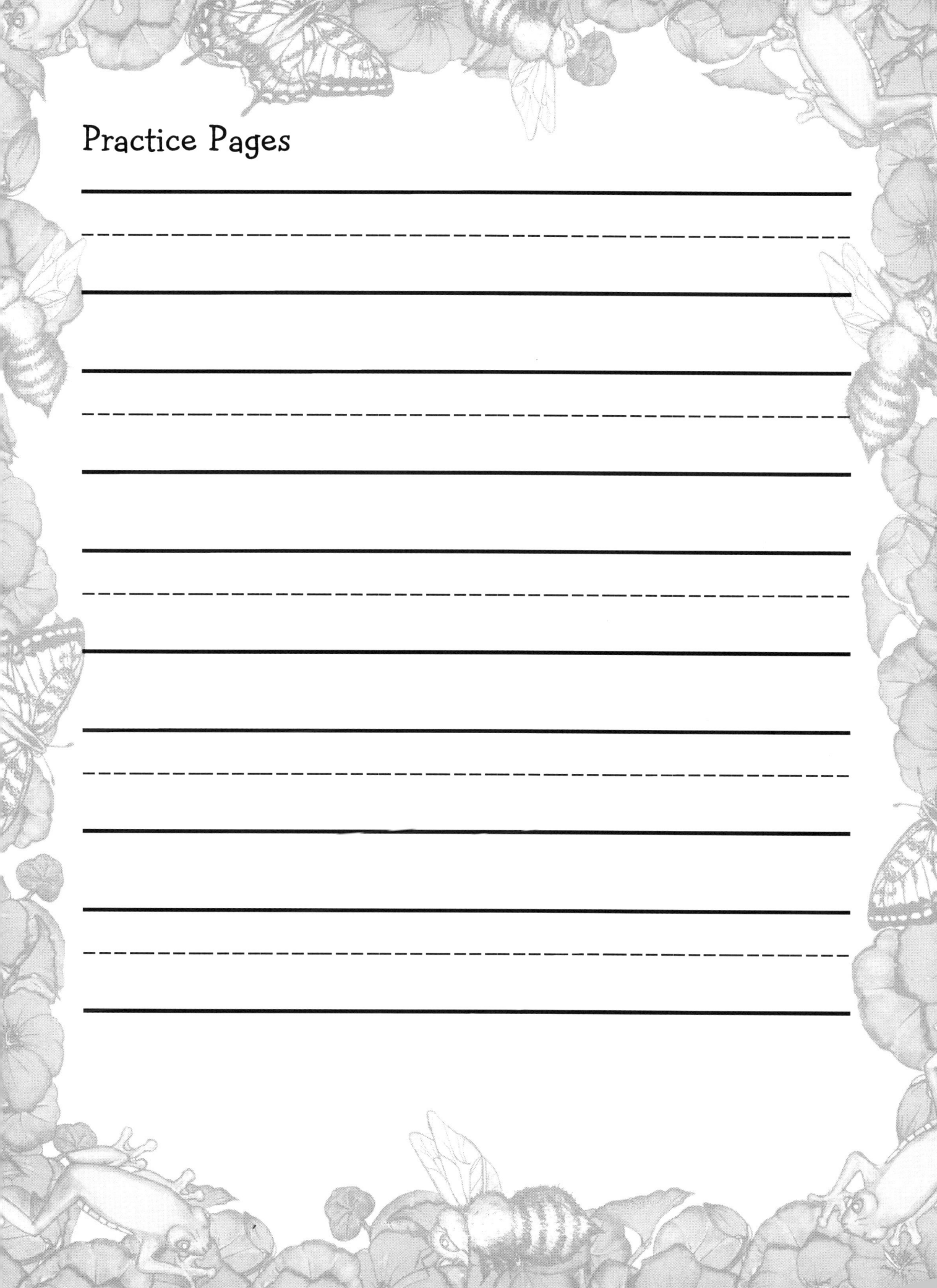

Practice Pages

Dr. Diana Carle earned her PhD in Entomology, a Bachelor of Science in Biology and Anthropology as well as a minor in Classics. However, her most impactful educational experience was the nature-based homeschool program she attended from kindergarten through 6th grade. From exploring and sketching life along the pond's edge, to observing the miracle of butterfly metamorphosis, she learned at a young age that no classroom was as captivating as the one created by God in nature. She has spent over 13 years in environmental research and STEM education, creating and delivering a wide range of hands-on science-based curricula for undergraduate, graduate, and adult professional education courses at Rutgers University. Dr. Carle has served as a research associate on the Nurture thru Nature project, a grade 3-12 after school and summer nature-based program aimed at bolstering students' scholastic performance and social development. She ran New Jersey's mosquito control training and certification program where she educated health department personnel on responsible mosquito control which conserves both human and environmental health. She also founded Insect Diva, a nature inspired jewelry company which provides public outreach on conservation education. provides public outreach on conservation education. Dr. Carle currently creates nature-based educational materials, writes and illustrates children's books, and manages two conservation projects in: Monarch Butterfly Conservation and Pollinator Habitat Restoration.

www.DoctorDianaCarle.com

Thank you so much for reading, I hope you experienced some of the wonder that learning in nature holds. If you are inspired to explore more about the natural world around us and how to use it as a learning resource, check out my other books, and join the mailing list by emailing me at:

DrDianaCarle@gmail.com

To Get Free Extras!

Title the email, "Nature's Living Classroom" And I'll send you a special guide with activities for learning in nature.

Made in the USA
Columbia, SC
23 November 2021